THE LIGHT
AT THE END OF DARKNESS

First Edition

ISBN 978-0-9793958-2-6
Text copyright 2010 © Salvador Jimenez
Front cover photograph copyright © 2010 by Ana Cristina Jimenez-Kimble

This is a Panoply Publishing product
panoplypublishing@me.com
Printed and bound in the United States

THE LIGHT
AT THE END OF DARKNESS

By
Salvador Jimenez

Panoply Publishing
Salt Lake City, UT USA

To God,
To my children and wife,
To my parents,
To my brothers and sisters
Thank You!

CONTENTS

ACKNOWLEDGMENTS

For someone like myself who is not a writer, to write a book can become an insurmountable task, especially when for practical reasons I decided to write it in English (Spanish being my first language).

On many occasions I felt facing a closed door for not knowing exactly what to do after I had completed a substantial part of my story. I didn't know if what I had written would be readable enough for English speakers or if the quality of what was to become my book would be acceptable for publishing.

It was at this point that I was fortunate to meet Rebecca Guevara, the accomplished author of *Write your Book*. After I told her my story and of my desire to publish my book, her response was of great encouragement - giving me her sound advice on how to proceed with such a difficult task, beginning with the application for the copyrights. At that moment I felt that the veil of my ignorance on this endeavor began to lift.

But Rebecca also gave me another amazing tip. She put me in contact with Susan Vogel, who at that moment was in the last stages of writing her own book, *Becoming Pablo O' Higgins*. As this story develops mainly in Mexico Rebecca thought I could help Susan with my views and comments, and Susan who is another accomplished writer, in reciprocity would help me with the grammar in my book.

This deal worked perfectly for both, but especially for me. Susan did a very serious revision of my manuscript, but at the same time gave me the wonderful idea to add some personal anecdotes of my life in Mexico to some chapters to give context

ACKNOWLEDGMENTS

to several concepts that seemed too remote. She also put me in contact with another great writer and editor, Andrea Moore-Emmet, who helped with the final editing.

My deepest gratitude goes out to these wonderful women. I also want to thank my family. My wife Claudia became very instrumental with her intelligent questions about several of my views in the book that were not clear to her. She is a perfectionist, as such she pushed me to give my best effort in clarifying those concepts until she would be satisfied with the structure of my conclusions. My daughter Ana Cristina who is very perceptive made me see that the general tone of my writing reflected me in the book as someone with an air of pomposity, something that by any means I would not want to portray. That led me to do a total revision of my manuscript along with her wise advise in mind. Also Ana Cristina and my son Ricardo, both helped with the last revision of my book.

Finally, I want to thank Rev. Dr. Phillip W. Zebley, an uncle of my wife, who despite his honest disagreements with some of my views concerning religion, nevertheless still gave me his valuable insight with which to balance my book.

PROLOGUE

I have only shared with my immediate family a life-changing experience I had when, at the age of sixteen I faced death. But now approaching the evening of my life, the time came for me to write about this amazing story.

I am sure that what happened to me at that crucial moment will be of interest to many people because I include in this story the detailed description of the different stages of the process of death, the most transcendental and feared event we all have to face at the end of our lives. But the most important element of this testimony is the incorporation of a complete description of our Creator as He appeared to me at the end of my amazing journey, the wonderful truth which deep down we hope to find. I also include how the empirical confirmation of this truth reshaped my perspective of the whole spectrum of life.

But I want to start explaining what became my purpose in life after my return and a brief description of who I am, as this is the background to this story. Through this, I hope those who read my book can picture the new person I became with the impact of the humbling experience and the opportunity granted to me with my return to this world.

The need to show my gratitude to God was the only motive of my return so it became my whole purpose in life. However, I have to confess with all honesty that in defining how I was going to accomplish such essential purpose with something of real value, was not easy for me. It took me several years and different approaches. In some instances, I even found myself going back to redefine my original purpose, especially when I was tempted by apparent "golden opportunities" in the business and social world in Mexico, where I come from. Fortunately I was able to redirect my life having seen that they were only distractions that would have taken me nowhere.

After much thinking about it, I finally decided that the best way to make use of my second opportunity in this life was to fully dedicate all my energy and my time in raising a family in the framework of the image and values of God, and at the same time that I would support my parents at their older age. The image I have of God as my Celestial Father was my clue to be able to decide that through my own family I would accomplish my main purpose in life. The beautiful example of my parents Salvador and Rosa Maria in the way they raised my siblings and me with their full love and commitment was also an important basis for reaching this fundamental decision.

In order to do this, after I graduated as a lawyer from the National Autonomous University of Mexico, UNAM, I became a member of the Mexican Foreign Service so I could have a stable job to support my family, and at the same time to be able to participate in a prestigious institution dealing with the international affairs of my country and with world peace. I also felt that I had to pay my debt to my country and to the world.

Despite being a very demanding job, and moving from one country to another mainly in Latin America with all the challenges and the opportunities of the diplomatic life, I have raised my family together with Claudia Kimble, my beautiful and loving wife for 34 years at this date, who I was lucky to meet her in

PROLOGUE

Washington D.C in my first assignment at the Organization of American States.

With our children Ricardo Esteban and Ana Cristina having graduated from college and now beginning their own lives, I have retired after 33 years in that fulfilling job to have time to write this book. Ricardo became a Doctor from Boston University and Ana Cristina graduated with a Masters degree in Speech Pathology from the University of Colorado. We couldn't be more proud of our children!

On the other side, the richness of the near-death experience transformed my perception of life and at the same time made me a more humble person, realizing how our reality in this world and our human dimension only makes sense when centered around the truth of this wonderful being as our loving Creator. The image of God for me is the driving force how I see the world. Maintaining this perspective, in the chapters ahead I analyze several concepts related to our human condition such as what is real happiness, our fear of death, consciousness, the appetite of power, ultimate justice, the concept of effort, the need to pray, and some others.

Thanks to my eye opening experience I also became well aware that God created the wonder of the universe with the absolutely precise conditions to breed our life. I can understand now how the seed of His own unique essence became incubated in our biological reality so we could reach the potential to become part of Him. I understand how in designing an evolved biological structure that is integrated with the intelligence

VII

achieved by our brain, our Creator not only establishes the basis for our knowledge to make sense of the universe and ourselves. Also in connection with our mind He allows us to reach the critical level of consciousness necessary to be ready to face our transcendental reality and destiny.

Based in the above perspective, I make use in my book of such empirical knowledge correlated with the pieces of knowledge attained by mankind that deal with our reality as individuals and with the reality that surrounds us. First from the perspective of religion in dealing with faith in God; as well as from the approach of physics and astrophysics that attempt to grasp the realities of the universe. This includes metaphysics, which from a philosophical approach overcomes the limitations of an isolated science that focuses only on nature and materialism to understand reality. Nature has several aspects that so far science has not been able to explain in a complete and convincing way.

With all due respect to the bright minds of science that have unveiled for mankind some of the great secrets of nature, we could not close our eyes to the fact that there are still many basic and important gaps to be filled in such endeavor. Not pretending by any means to measure up myself to the giants of science, I still feel that I should make a humble contribution in the understanding of nature and the universe in the framework of our Creator.

However, I have to clarify that I am perfectly aware of my limitations in this tremendous challenge of writing this book. Sometimes it scares me to think how it was that I dared to deal with these difficult subjects in the different areas examined when I should have been better prepared with much more years of formal education (especially for having written it in English considering that Spanish is my first language). My total determination to not depart from this world without leaving my written testimony for others was the motivation that overcame my fears.

On the other hand, I anticipate that some people will not agree with my views nor believe what I describe of my experience. In my life, I have seen that for any view that is exposed, there is always someone who will refute it. The quality of the argument tends not to matter, as there will always be someone who does not agree. This is part of our human nature.

The central point of my story is a testimony supporting a fact and not a supposition or a theory. I am not looking to promote any confrontational debate. My only purpose is to share in good faith and with all honesty the wonderful experience I had, which for me has been an awakening of fundamental value. For the same reason I believe someone else could also benefit by defining better his or her transcendental purpose in learning and growing from it. If that were the case, then my effort in sharing my story in this book would be completely rewarded.

I should not forget to mention that I am aware that several other people have gone through similar experiences and have returned to life on earth after facing death. For this reason there are some similarities in our stories. As an example, there are many descriptions of people traveling through a tunnel where they see a very bright light at the end. I can associate with this description, more precisely at the point when I felt an enormous force of attraction driving me at a tremendous speed to meet with a wonderful being of light and energy. The speed and movement that I experienced could be interpreted as the perception of those people describing how they were traveling through a tunnel towards that light.

Another coincidence is in the description I make in my book of the process of absorption that takes place at the pinnacle of death comparing it with a drop of rain falling into the ocean.

I must say that I consider myself just an ordinary human being. I would not pretend to feel special or any different than others who tell us their valuables stories about death. If I some-day met another person who had gone as far as I did in the process of his or her death, I am sure that we would happily agree with each other one hundred percent in the description of what we experienced. In our final destiny the Truth is only one!

At the end of this book I decided to add a chapter with my views about the crossroads for humankind as a complement of this effort. The fundamental notion about God continue to be under attack by the materialistic approach to life despite all the irrefutable evidence of a Creator of the universe. This rejection to accept God, combined with the mentality of self sufficience and power derived from the explosion of knowledge with no moral direction, is taking humankind to the wrong perception of reality. It is my personal desire that the empirical knowledge I gained in my experience with death, which I want to share in this book, could somehow help humankind to become aware of the tremendous risk of getting lost in the darkness for taking the road without God.

PART ONE

A TRANSFORMATIONAL EXPERIENCE

"The call of death is a call of love. Death can be sweet if we answer it in the affirmative, if we accept it as one of the great eternal forms of life and transformation."

\- Herman Hesse

"When it is dark enough you can see the stars."

- Ralph Waldo Emerson

C H A P T E R   1

MY JOURNEY, MY RETURN

As a son of a miner I learned to adapt to the special kind of life of a person with the spirit of adventure who is determined to strike rich in the silver mines wherever they are. That meant having to follow my father Salvador to different remote places in Mexico. Such a way of life did not necessarily appeal to my mother Rosa Maria, who would have preferred stability rather than having to move from one place to another every year. But I did not have a problem with that. I inherited my father's genes and enjoyed the adventure of travel and discovering new places, especially when my father took me with him in his yellow jeep to explore the mines.

However when the economic situation would turn really bad--which happened on many occasions, my parents had no other option but to send my brother Guillermo and me to live with my grandmother Isabel (already a widow at that time) and my aunts Ana and Mercedes who owned a chicken farm in Mexico City until things would improve. My oldest sister, Maria Antonieta, was sent to live with my grandmother Ana Munoz, my mother's mother. My brother Hector and my sisters Susana and Pili were too young to be separated, and so remained with my parents.

I missed my parents but I also enjoyed living with my grandmother and aunts. They also were adventurous in another measure. We used to have picnics at a pass between the two huge snow-covered volcanos that can be seen from the city, the Popocatepetl and the Ixtlacihuatl. The place is called Paso Cortez in remembrance of the Spanish conqueror Hernan Cortez who came to Mexico City (then Technotitlan) through the pass. Imagine an older and dignified woman struggling to climb. We all had to pull and push her, but she held on very stoically and never gave up!

My grandmother had another virtue that I enjoyed in particular. She was the best cook of traditional Mexican food. She used to make a special mushroom soup that was the main attraction for family and friends who always begged her to prepare it for dinner. I was the first among them. It was made with pork meat and chiles poblanos. But of course the main ingredient and the secret of its success was the wild mushrooms that we picked at the base of the volcanos growing under the shade of the pine trees. That was one of the reasons for her asking to be taken to those places. Such delicious soup was out of this world and it was worth the special effort!

But I remember the famous soup not only because it was a true delicacy with the most delicious taste. It almost became my last dinner and was a factor in the most important event in my whole life. At the time the event took place I was only sixteen but I remember every portion of my experience in the most vivid detail.

I was enjoying the soup for dinner when at the moment I began to swallow, I felt with repugnance a clump of cat hair (there were thirteen cats living in the house that were allowed to walk on the kitchen table) passing down my throat. I had no other choice but to swallow it because I did not want to spit it on the table.

Immediately I could feel how my throat with a strong spasm closed completely due to a powerful anaphylactic allergic reaction to the cat hair. But, at that point I was not yet alarmed, because at that young age I used to dive and compete with some friends to see who could hold their breath the longest underwater. I usually won with a personal record of two minutes, so I remained calm, trusting that I was going to hold until the situation passed. My brother Guillermo, however, who was next to me, noticed what was going on and handed me a glass of water to clear my throat. But my throat did not open at all, so finally I had to spit the water on the table.

More than the two minutes had passed - maybe three without me being able to breathe. At that moment everything turned around. It was brutally evident to me that I had gone beyond my mark of two minutes. I really started to feel the terror and pain as if my lungs were going to rip open through my chest. A true desperation came upon me because at that point there was no doubt in my mind that I was facing death. My previous macho stance went down the drain!

Out of control, my reaction was to stand violently from my chair, stretching my neck as much as I could as if that action were going to help open my throat. But to no avail. What I was facing at that moment is no doubt one of the worst ways of dying, at least that is how I felt at that moment of agony. My strongest instinct, the instinct of survival, was demanding from my body to battle and resist to the limit, but it looked like the battle was lost.

Up to that point I felt a horrible combination of extreme pain, terror and desperation, being brutally aware of the crude reality of death. With my macho dignity being defeated, every cell of my body made me feel that for sure it was the end of my days. At that moment, clinging to the last breath of life, into my mind from nowhere came the image of the cross, which undeniably gave me the moral support that I desperately needed in those difficult moments. At that crucial stage, no doubt the hardest we experience through the whole process of dying with the combination of physical and moral pain, I was able to feel what it means to have faith, and how it helps us.

But then things began to change. First, I started seeing blurry as if I was in a dense milky fog. Then abruptly, I sensed a total disconnection from my body, as if someone had turned off a switch. I could not feel my body any more, a rare sensation, but at the same time with a sense of relief because my need to breath seemed to disappear completely. At that moment I said to myself, "well, I am dying but after all it is not so bad, at least I am not suffering pain any more". Maybe that situation could be compared with the anesthesia we receive in the operating room. We do not feel our body or any pain, but the big difference in this kind of experience was that I did not lose consciousness. Under the effects of anesthesia we do not even dream (I have gone through two operations so I can attest to this).

Next, I went through the point where I remembered my life but in very quick succession, like a movie at full speed. That made me realize how short my life had been. I was convinced at that point that at any moment I was going to die completely and lose consciousness - a reasonable thought because after all I was dying.

But I remained in that condition. I had not vanished nor lost consciousness. The fog gave way to total darkness. I was entering into another stage. But I could sense that the total darkness that surrounded me not only was lack of light but something different. It was the Nothing. Absolute emptiness! I could not hear anything, see anything nor feel anything. And of course I did not feel the need to breathe anymore to continue life in that immaterial condition. All that was there was me (my soul), nothing else but with my consciousness expanded many times more than in my normal life, making me amazingly aware of the very odd condition in which I was suspended.

Of course I reacted with perplexity. There was not the slightest doubt in my mind that I was dying but at the same time, ironically, I was more keenly aware of the reality of myself than at any other occasion. It was like my mind was evolving to another level, reaching its full potential of consciousness (obviously I was aware of that, too). The fact was that I definitely felt dead, but I had not disappeared into nothingness. With this conviction in my mind, the shocking idea of becoming extinguished with death went away.

Moreover, at the same time I was convinced that I didn't need my body anymore to continue living. I realized at such moment that I had left my material life to become a new kind of entity to continue living. It was not an ending and it was more than a continuum. It was a new phase.

That could be the reason why I was in total bewilderment but with no fear. But then I asked myself the big question if that was it, if the absolute nothingness that surrounded me would continue forever, if that odd situation could become my permanent new reality: me, myself, all alone, suspended in that void. With those hard questions in my mind my previous state of calm started to give way to a certain feeling of anguish, yet somehow I still maintained my faith in a positive outcome of the situation.

What was very clear to me was that I didn't want to remain in that reality alone by myself and things should change somehow. That's what I felt clinging to my faith!

It was at that precise instant that things began to change again. I sensed that something else appeared there in that nothingness, something extremely small, almost imperceptible, but I could sense it was there somewhere.

Despite my obvious lack of eyesight and use of my brain, I could sense it with great clarity with my consciousness. First as a very tiny particle of concentrated energy and then as light, but at the same time it was growing and growing in intensity in an explosive fashion, until there was a moment that I realized something amazing. It was a "being" not a "thing" and I could sense the reality and the presence of that being with the same clarity that my expanded mind was able to make me conscious of myself. In the middle of that void there were now only two realities, the being that appeared in the nothingness and me!

I paid great attention to what was happening, to the fact that in the middle of that absolute emptiness I was not alone anymore. But obviously a new question came to my mind, who could be that being there coming to meet me?

Whoever he was he continued growing, but I noticed that he was growing very rapidly and at the same time he was approaching me at an incredible speed coming from very far away. And the closer the being was to me, the more clearly I could sense his overwhelming tremendous dimension, realizing that he was an extremely powerful being of infinite energy.

At the same time that this unknown entity of tremendous energy was coming towards me I also felt I was being pulled to him with an immense and overpowering force. The light emanating from that being had substance and was beginning to touch me, and I could feel how he was beginning to absorb me in his own essence. It was not an abstract entity by any means, nor a spirit in the human conception we have of a spiritual entity. Its substance was real, more real than anything in spite of not being made of the material substance we see in this world. I became aware that the nature of his substance was made of energy, but at the same time much more complex because that energy was a living energy with qualitative elements like intelligence and harmony. A mind that was beginning to take form! That's why I could make the distinction between the "thing" that initially I had perceived as such and the "being" who was in front of me. It was something almost beyond description. It was like getting close to an enormous celestial object like the sun and I could feel his immense power, the radiance, the pulling forces, and the energy in front of me. It was the most overwhelming feeling I had ever experienced!

It was at that moment in front of that towering entity, that I could realize something else, that I was made of the same essence as he. At that advanced point into the process of my death my consciousness made me well aware that I shared his essence of living energy, his same defining elements in the conformation of this being. I had been striped from my material body, but in this new reality I remained with my subsisting mind and own energy. This is how I was able to identify with him when he was beginning to touch me. However, with a clear distinction, in reality nothing or anybody could compare to His infinite dimension and majesty!

The same awareness not only totally dissipated any fears in me, but more importantly it made me understand at that moment many basic questions about myself and humankind, the cause and purpose of the reality of the universe, and more importantly, the meaning of our life and death linked to our destiny. I became the most humble being when at that point I finally could understand and confirm the reality behind such amazing truths.

At that moment I was able to unveil with a single stroke the whole truth behind those fundamental subjects debated here on earth, as it should happen to everybody else who reaches that point.

I was in front of my destiny, nothing was in between. Moreover, I began to feel how I was starting the process of becoming absorbed into the essence of that amazing entity. It was at this precise moment, in a state of absolute happiness and having reached my full level of consciousness, that I finally could comprehend the whole truth about whom I was encountering:

This majestic being is God!

He is our Creator, our source!

We share His own essence!

He is our destiny, our ultimate reality!

We are going to be totally absorbed in His own essence so we become part of Him!

We have to leave our material bodies through our deaths to reach Him in His own realm!

He does not demand anything from us!

He does not put any conditions on us!

He gives us everything: His love and absolute happiness in Himself!

He is an entity of living energy in a perfect combination of intelligence and harmony!

He is infinitely powerful!

His ultimate essence is love!

It is important to take into account that my state at that moment was of total disconnection with my body and my corporal senses. However what subsisted of me, my vital energy with my consciousness, my soul, was all that was necessary to be aware of God and face Him in his full majesty and reality. It is perfectly reasonable to understand that if we were to keep our regular biological bodies when facing God with His immense power and energy that emanates from Him, we would be totally obliterated into a thousand pieces. The process of our deaths is a cleansing and transformational process for our adaptation to a new form of life.

This should explain why we have to die in the material sense of the word. We have to leave our material bodies in this world through the process of death so we can reach the higher condition, the potentiality, that will make it possible to face God in His unique realm and to become one with Him in His own essence.

I have been asked how I perceived this process of absorption in the substance of God, if such occurrence could be compared to a living cell which becomes part of an organism. The way I can describe it is more as if we were a drop of rain falling into the ocean. When we reach its surface, we become absorbed and transformed into the greatness of the ocean. The absorption is absolute and we become merged in a holistic reality. But in this wonderful case I am talking about an Ocean of Love!

Now, how is it that I am back in this world, having been at the gateway of Heaven? What would explain this unique situation, was that at such moment of absolute happiness, at the brink of my complete absorption into the substance of God which was already taking place, spontaneously I felt a humble and honest feeling that what I was receiving from God, my eternal life with Him, was so beautiful and so immense that I needed to reciprocate somehow. I realized at that last moment that I had previously wasted my short life on earth without giving to it any real purpose.

I needed another opportunity, so with all my sincerity I asked my Father, "Please give me one more minute of my life on earth to show my gratitude and my own love to you." I wanted to say thanks!

His response was instantaneous. Like an electric jolt I felt I was regaining my body again with an unpleasant sensation of cold and heaviness. I was back in this world! In total amazement of what had happened I opened my eyes and could see my brother Guillermo, my grandmother and my aunts staring at me lying on the floor with a scared look reflected in their faces. They told me that they were convinced that I was dead after more than five minutes had passed since I had collapsed on the floor.

I got up with the help of my brother, and started to worry how I was going to be able to accomplish something of value for God in that short time. I really was convinced that I was going to have only the one minute I had asked from Him. But after more than five minutes, I began to feel comforted that God was going to give me more time for my opportunity to accomplish my purpose.

In addition to the one minute that I asked God for, with His generosity He has so far conceded me forty eight years more in this world since I went through that amazing experience in the process of my death. I am still here trying to accomplish my purpose in this life on earth because in His infinite love, He listened to me!

I don' t know when, but I am certain that it will be sooner rather than later when God decides it is time I will again take the journey to encounter Him.

I know that anything I could have accomplished to show Him my gratitude for everything I have received from His love will never be enough, not even if it had taken me a million years trying to achieve such purpose. However, I trust that our Creator is going to be pleased with what I humbly will bring Him the next time I am reunited with Him for eternity for having used every minute as if it were the last. All I want is to show Him my sincere gratitude with my entire life. And, of course, I will also have to add my thanks for the second opportunity I got!

"I would maintain that thanks is the highest form of thought; and that gratitude is happiness doubled by wonder."
- G.K. Chesterton

CHAPTER 2

MY OPPORTUNITY TO THANK GOD

The reason I came back to this world when I was reaching the point of no return at the precise moment I began to be absorbed in the substance of God was that a spontaneous need was born in me to express my gratitude to Him. At that amazing opportunity of facing my Creator I was able to feel and understand all the meaning of His immense and unconditional love towards me.

Overwhelmed, I said to myself looking back at my short life I had lived on earth: "Wait a moment, how is it that I am receiving this wonderful gift of the love of God when I have not done anything to show this amazing Being not even a little bit of what He is giving me?"

In having this thought, I felt a strong need, an urge, to do whatever was within my reach to show how grateful I was for the striking significance of everything coming to my mind at that moment of truth. It was as if I had been invited to a great reception and the owner of the residence came to open the door to greet me inviting me to join the wonderful party inside, but at that moment I realized that I did not bring any present.

I have to say that all this was not born in me at that moment because I felt God was asking anything from me in return as a condition, or because of a feeling of fear or guilt in me. Not at all. On the contrary, it was born precisely because I was touched very profoundly by the extreme purity of the essence of the love of God that I was already receiving in fullness. I was given everything, but He had not asked for anything in return.

The overwhelming emotion in my initial encounter with my Father was a combination of astonishment and deep admiration produced by the most tremendous power and energy that He projected over me, as if I were in front of the biggest celestial object in the universe. At that precise moment I knew unambiguously who created us together with the universe. That emotion exploded in joy when I felt His love and it became clear to me that I am a product of this love.

The resulting feeling can only be described as absolute happiness! Actually, I also perceived something subliminal and reassuring, His own joy and happiness for having me. It was as if He knew I was coming and was expecting me. In this situation could anyone ask for more?

That was when, totally overwhelmed and completely aware that I was already stepping in my new and ultimate reality, absorbed in the same essence of my Father for eternity, I said with all my sincerity, "Please give me one more minute of my life on earth to show you my gratitude and my own love to you". And here I am!

Obviously in asking to return to this world to be able to accomplish such desire, tacitly I had already accepted to merge in the essence of God, and I trusted, beyond any shadow of a doubt, that once I completed my purpose, He would bring me back to complete my journey to Heaven.

As I said before, at the moment of writing this book, forty-eight years have gone by since my return. Somehow I think that if it had been only the one minute that I had in mind, I really don't know what I could have accomplished with that short time. My wishful interpretation, considering that sixty seconds make one minute, is that what actually happened was that God in His wisdom and generosity extended that particular concept of one minute with sixty seconds, to sixty years instead. So that way I could have plenty of time to accomplish my purpose. That would mean that I still have ahead twelve more years to live in this world. That is what I think.

But whatever the total time is that I am going to have in my return to earth, I am determined to continue using it to thank God every minute of my life as if it were the last.

I will continue doing, as I have done so far, after having granted my return, saying thank you to God every single day, every single moment, but also making sure that with my concrete actions I am participating in God's project for humanity. In other words, in living intensely and fully every moment of my life in the framework of His image of love with my own project, my family.

This does not mean that I pretend to become a saint, or even near saintly. I am well aware of my shortcomings and my many imperfections that make of me an ordinary human being. All I want is to manifest my humble gratitude with all my strength and every portion of my soul, living my life to the completion of my time on Earth to grow as a true child of God, but stepping into real life with all its challenges.

I remember when I told my grandmother Isabel of what I had gone through when she witnessed my near-death experience, she advised me to become a Father (in the Catholic church the priests are called Father). I responded yes, but a father of many children. She didn't think that was very funny!

Raising a family these days in this troubled world is no doubt a big challenge, but it is my belief that it is also a wonderful opportunity to express in a concrete form my appreciation to God, participating this way in His project for humanity. I want to make absolutely sure that He knows that his love towards me is producing in reciprocity something concrete and real in me of the same kind, infinite love towards Him. So in my need and desire to say thanks I am loving God too, participating in the process of His creation of life in this world.

In responding to the obvious question of why I was able to return to life on earth after my close encounter with God, when nobody else seems to have gone through the same fabulous experience of having reached that far and returned, I strongly believe that the spontaneous feeling that was produced in me at that moment allowed my return to this world. Not because it came to me as something special or different from what most others have experienced in their own process of death. What maybe took place differently (this is my educated guess) could have been that I asked for another opportunity to thank God just at the very last instant before the point of no return, just at the last moment before completing the process of death merging totally in His essence. If I had hesitated, I would not be here now writing this book.

I am convinced that the many people who have died since the beginning of time, who have gone through the same process of death realizing at that moment they wasted their lives, have had the same need to thank God as a consequence of their awareness and love to Him at that final moment, but evidently they must have crossed by then the point of no return. I reacted an instant before, that must have been the only difference.

But regardless of that, they still will complete their journey being absorbed in God. Our celestial Father will welcome them anyway, I have no doubt of that. And I think this way, because I am also convinced that our Father created all of His children the same, with the same virtues and value. Our celestial Father loves us the same, and will respond to us the same.

Obviously the main reason why many others do not return is simply because they must have already used their lives in accomplishing their purpose. They don't have to ask to return. They are the immense majority of people who have not wasted their life not as I had wasted mine until the moment I had my eye opening experience with death.

On the other hand I also believe that our desire to express our gratitude comes as a natural need when we realize that the purpose of our creation, our existence and the potential of our life in this world has only one outcome, our absolute happiness when we become absorbed in God. It would be difficult to imagine how not to say thanks to our Creator, when in saying thanks implicitly we are saying yes, I accept what you are giving me and I value it very highly.

This is why I believe that anyone who reaches the necessary level of consciousness is aware of what it means to encounter eternal life, love and happiness with God. Our mind will necessarily produce this natural sentiment of acceptance and appreciation saying thanks.

I also have been thinking why I felt the need to come back to this world in order to thank God from here when I could have waited an instant more and expressed the same sentiment when being together with my Creator in my new reality.

I am sure our Father would have valued this sentiment the same as it must happen with all those others who, without any pause, complete the process of death and get together with Him. However I believe that the opportunity we have with our life in our material reality in this world is mostly as individual entities, as the human beings we are, with individual souls and our own consciousness.

Not only that, in this world we are a mixture of matter and souls subjected to the forces and the complex phenomena of nature resulting in what we become in this life, humans, with all the virtues and all our defects as such.

So thanking God while we are living in this material world represents a special challenge because we are subjected to the shortcomings and temptations imbedded in our human dimension which we have to overcome to reach our potential. This factor should confer a special meaning and value to our action of showing our gratitude to our Father.

This is the reason why our life in this world as human entities is a wonderful opportunity but a challenge at the same time. Our soul has to mix with our body and brain which are functioning matter, our biological element. From the level of harmonic combination of one element with the other we become individual entities defined as humans, nevertheless still one step from becoming perfect entities.

This is how God created us. This is why we live in this particular universe, in this particular dimension of energy, matter and space-time, so we can be individual human entities with the potential to become a complete and higher entity when we become united with our Father.

If we can be aware of this fact, then we can direct our life to a transcendental purpose that will drive us to our final destiny together with God. But in this awareness we should also see the big opportunity to start thanking God without delay, so we don't waste any time in justifying our individual reality in our ephemeral transit through this world. This is one of the tremendous lessons I learned with my experience in facing death. This is what I wanted to share in this book.

I hope people who have an interest in reading about my near-death experience consider also the special opportunity of using every minute of their lives to accomplish their own purpose of thanking and loving God. This way at the moment of getting together with our Father we all can finish our journey in peace with the complete satisfaction of bringing Him, as a present, our life on earth!

"Integrity is telling myself the truth. And honesty is telling the truth to other people."

- Spencer Johnson

CHAPTER 3

AN HONEST QUESTION, AN HONEST ANSWER

In my first experience at preschool when I was just a little boy I faced a situation that made me ask why my school friends didn't like me. They treated me with rejection and made me feel different. At that time my father who was a miner had taken the family to the city of Ciudad Obregon in Sonora in the search of precious minerals. I was only three years old and it was where I got my first memories of life.

Most of my friends as most of the Mexicans living in that small town at that moment had their skin darker than mine. Both my parents belong to the nine percent of white people in Mexico and I was extremely white. At least that's how I felt in contrast with my friends. But I felt weird because everybody made me feel different.

However later on in life while studying at the university in

Mexico City, ironically this contrast worked to my advantage with girls who belonged to the high society in Mexico where white people are more prevalent. I felt different again, but this time because the doors of the privileged in Mexico were opened to me. From there I easily jumped to the world of high business and big economic opportunities, which at that time in my life posed a serious challenge to my purpose. I had to face some compromising moral dilemmas which could have taken me in a different direction of my main purpose in life.

But the fact is that I felt different all the time when living in my own country, a psychological and social reference that could have made me believe that I was special.

To all that I have to add my unique experience with death, one more reason to feel that I was special. In regard to this the honest question I ask myself is how is it that I was permitted to return to this world when I was beginning to step in the other dimension where God is taking us to become one with Him? I frankly have had the thought that the meaning of my return could have occurred because I could had been chosen for a special purpose.

Taking into account that the special experience I went through the process of my death was unique in the registered history of mankind considering how far I went into it, and adding to the fact that so far in my search I have not met anybody having had a near death experience reaching that advanced stage. So it would seem logical to think in the remote possibility that I possibly was chosen for a particular reason.

Of course there are several elements of coincidence that others have experienced in their near death experiences that I also perceived, like the separation of our body, a sensation of calm in spite of the fact that we are dying, the perception of a bright light, but especially keeping the capacity of awareness despite our dying bodies.

What I have not been able to find is the description of the sequence of the different stages, nor the details and precise analysis of the different elements I encountered in the various phases of the phenomena. One important stage missing in other descriptions is the moment when I was in an absolute void that I could describe as "the nothing" and what happened when, having identified in the middle of that nothingness a minuscule thing. A moment later and getting closer that object turned out to be a "being" and not "a thing." My deduction is that other people in their near death experiences have not reached that far so they can't give us an account of this advanced stage.

Furthermore, the "light" others describe only as a simple light in terms of our physical reality. It is not the kind of light which for example we could see in a flash light. It is nothing else than a "being" made up of an overpowering energy, a living energy, that is perceived by our mind as light but in the last instance the substance of that light is a special and wonderful combination of energy, love, intelligence and harmony. We see the Light!

At that moment we become enlightened. We become illuminated by this overwhelming truth. So the light we see at that amazing moment cannot be compared with the physical light we see in this world. Such light is a more complete and complex substance. It is the substance of God.

For this reason having been there at that far point into the process of death, I think it is conceivable that the extent and the uniqueness of the phenomena I experienced through such process could have had a special significance that could have driven me to the wrong interpretation that I was chosen to do something special for others.

But nothing like that could have taken place with me. I have to be honest with myself, I am not the kind of person who can make a fool of himself and I don't have any interest in wasting my life with false pretensions.

As I have explained before in a spontaneous reaction to my overwhelming feeling of gratitude to God that was born in me at the pinnacle of the moment of truth, I asked God to give me one more minute of my life on earth to do something that could be my tangible demonstration of my love for Him. The fact that My Father responded to my petition is just one more proof of His infinite love for me, but at the same time it is very clear to me that my return did not obey to any indication of doing anything on behalf of my Creator nor did I receive any message or revelation of any kind. It was only a response of love to an honest and spontaneous petition.

My return is just another tangible demonstration that God listens to us when we ask with our hearts. In responding to me instantaneously and without any hesitation He allowed me to have the opportunity with no conditions to redirect my life to a transcendental purpose as it was my purest desire.

For the same reason and having evaluated with all honesty the significance of my second opportunity in my return to this world, I am certain that my amazing experience did not imply any special responsibilities of conveying special messages to anyone. I reached the happy conclusion that I was going to have the freedom to choose with no limitations or conditions on how I was going to achieve my purpose. God gave me the freedom of choice with no strings attached!

Once I concluded the above, I went for a long and difficult period of search and trial and error to determine what could be a project of real value in the eyes of God that He would take as a token of my gratitude and love for him. After I dismissed some apparent opportunities, my final decision was to have a family with its foundations grounded in accordance with the project of God for us. Everything else that I would do while I was to remain in this world would be directed exclusively to the support of my central project, my family. I wanted to make absolutely sure that I wouldn't waste my second opportunity.

But not withstanding the above I have to say that I do believe that God has conveyed special messages to humankind with some of his Chosen Children through various critical periods of our history. Some of those special messengers have been the prophets and messiahs who are very well known and every solid religion is identified and defined by their own. As a common denominator those chosen by God for that purpose have received their messages in critical times of history to be transmitted to humankind for particular reasons that God determines important in helping our civilization to find the road that goes to Him. They bring to us the Light and the Truth, obviously adapted to their particular times and to the cultural environments and psychological mentalities of their regional communities. This has produced the different faiths of the world. While their message in general contains many of the fundamental elements that I had the fortune to identify and confirm through the process of my death, my particular experience is of a specific nature, a phenomenon that cannot be compared in any measure with the important and special dimension of the mission of these respectful champions of religion. Theirs is the word of God. Mine is just a personal and circumstantial testimony of an ordinary human being.

I believe that God created us with an intelligence housed in our bodies in the brain combined with our mind so we can reach the level of consciousness necessary for the comprehension of His reality and His love towards us. But occasionally, in a constructive time sequence, He sends to us messages of a moral value that complement our own capacity to be aware of his existence so we can comprehend better the dimension of His love to mankind.

Those messages carried by these special Children of God are the pillars of the different faiths that we know around the world which were built with their particular psychological and cultural perspectives to serve the common divine purpose of showing humanity the road towards the Light. With this conviction in mind, I pay my sincere respects to the different churches of the world dedicated to helping humankind find the road to its transcendental purpose.

This is something that I have to recognize and appreciate greatly, but only in the position of an ordinary and humble human being with lots of imperfections and shortcomings, and not as someone special or with the capacity to judge others.

Moreover, I could not deny that making use of those happy conclusions about religion, the significance and value of my particular experience in the process of my death became reinforced and confirmed to its fullest extent in the rich knowledge that I gained. Later on in another chapter I will delve deeper into this subject.

In any case, if there is a reason for me to feel special it is only because I am a child of God. The same as the several billion other children of God who live in this world including those we have yet to meet in the future who must live in other regions of the vast universe!

"Sharing knowledge is not about giving people something, or getting something from them. That is only valid for information sharing. Sharing knowledge occurs when people are interested in helping one another develop new capacities for action; it is about creating learning processes."

- Peter Senge

CHAPTER 4

MY MOTIVES IN WRITING THIS EXPERIENCE

I am getting closer to the moment of my departure. Looking in retrospect at that moment, when lying on the floor after returning from the eye opening experience in my encounter with death, I wonder how much more time I still will have on this earth to continue fulfilling my purpose. It is not only that I can count the many years I have on my shoulders, but there are many other undeniable signs that tell me that the end for me could be around the corner.

After having reached 65, I begin to feel the weight of time in many ways. My movements are slower, it takes me longer to start my activities in the mornings, my knees and my elbows hurt, and the names of friends and events are becoming harder to remember. What really concerns me is that my doctor indicated I had to start taking some medications for the prostrate and to lower my cholesterol despite a good diet and daily exercise. I no longer feel the pride I have felt all my life in having great health and not taking any medicine.

That is how I feel in view of my age and because time seems to accelerate as I grow older, so I could not miss the opportunity to write about the wonderful empirical knowledge that I gained in my near death experience confirming what every human being must know very deeply in their minds. That God exists, that He is our creator and the creator of the universe where we are nested, that this material life is only a step to reach our final destiny to be together with God in eternity, that all the beauty and immensity of the universe comes from God as an expression of His essence of energy, intelligence, harmony and love. I honestly cannot think of any other piece of knowledge of such importance for us so I would not leave this world without sharing it with everybody else.

I am convinced that we all are in the position of having this awareness because of our capacity of consciousness that God gave us through the combination of our senses with our intelligence and mind, and of course, through the fundamental role of religion. We have at our disposition several ways to be aware of God. All that is needed is our will to see and accept Him. However the kind of empirical knowledge that I brought back to this world with me, at least to my understanding, is one more

31

evidence that confirms that our life only makes sense linked to our transcendental destiny.

Besides wanting to share with everyone the different stages I found through the process of my death, I also would like to analyze the significance of my life in reference to my transcendental purpose defined on the basis of such experience. I believe that sharing the enriching experience I went through and the important reference that it gave to my life could be of help to someone else interested in the analysis and definition of his or her own purpose in life. It is tremendously important not to waste the opportunity to pursue our transcendental purpose, especially considering that life is so precious and time so short, and death can come at any moment.

On the other hand, what one could define as his own purpose does not necessarily have to be the same as others. The vastness of the project of God in the creation of Man is such that there will be many opportunities for anyone to find something of value in the eyes of God.

In my particular quest some elements became essential. First, my will to do it (implies a choice, a decision), the definition of my project, a plan to achieve it, and of course, getting into action with full determination. But I think that the most important of these elements is our will. Without our desire to express ourselves to God there would be nothing even if we achieve things by inertia.

Of course, I do not want to let pass the opportunity and my need of sharing with everybody through this book my amazing feeling of wonder and joy, combined with a profound emotion when at the end of the process of my death I encountered God. Nothing is comparable. The feeling is overpowering and at the same time subliminal. Just imagine being able to confirm the most important news of our lives! We keep existing but not at the same level as before. In that absorption with God we reach a level of existence at which there are not words to describe it. I rejoice just thinking when I was beginning to merge into that reality with God what we have been expecting, thanks in part to our faith, but at that moment is confirmed through our expanded level of consciousness.

That level of awareness, combined with our faith in God, becomes a concrete and marvelous new reality through the process of our death. On the other hand, we realize that our fears everything will end with death, are dissipated completely and are replaced with total confidence. No more fears. But we discover something wonderful at the moment when we face God in all his glory; and that is our own transformation into the same essence of God, essentially his essence of love. This would explain how it is possible that we can be absorbed finally by Him. I can only describe all these emotions combined in two words: absolute happiness!

So this adds to my motivation in writing about all this amazing empirical knowledge I gained. If someone has any fears or doubts about death I would like that person to look at my experience as solid evidence that tells everything about our final destiny. A destiny of eternal life and happiness and not a destiny of

SALVADOR JIMENEZ

extinction and darkness as we could fear.

This is my honest testimony. We must not be afraid of death. God is waiting for us with all its wonderful implications at the end of this wonderful journey!

Another helpful conviction I want to share is about my certainty that my loved ones here on earth, my family; including my parents, brothers and sisters eventually will all be reunited and absorbed in God in our final destiny. That is also the destiny for all humankind. This is an additional reason to eliminate our concerns that we fear and the grief for the separation with the passing of our dearest people at the end of their lives in this world. Death will reunite us with our celestial Father for eternity to celebrate happiness all together! What else could we ask for?

It is also very important for me to describe how I have learned to calibrate my mind to see and enjoy the world with an amplified point of view thanks to my enriching experience. I have been able to understand that life as a whole is a unitary concept made of different elements that integrate in harmony. As it is even with the most elementary particles that make up the universe as it is with God.

Also the way I see life now is not only from the angle of our material reality. Instead, I apply the multidimensional perspective I learned in the process of my death integrating in harmony a total reality of both dimensions; the material world where we live now and the new one where we are going when we die. This way I can evaluate my actions better with two interrelated elements of reference. I could describe it as a two dimensional perspective of my life giving me a solid reference to have a more truthful image of myself. I am not only the image of my body reflected in a mirror or the material image that other people can see of me. Simultaneously, I try to see me in the eyes of God so I have a better idea of who I really am.

Moreover, this way of seeing things has driven me to expand my interest in learning because I try to find the interconnections of one piece of knowledge with another. In other words, I do not see things isolated per se. Even in the most remote corner of the universe if we move an atom, that change will have an effect in another part of the universe.

I have translated all this as a methodology in my process of understanding new knowledge and I want to share it with anyone who could find it useful. In my case this methodology has helped me to find some very interesting angles of knowledge that allows me to fully enjoy learning.

However, I have to humbly recognize that not everybody would agree with me, as was the case with some professors of physics who rejected this approach to science in my years at the university in Mexico. I do not have the illusion that my conclusions will convince many other people to believe that I am right, but I want to share them anyway because I am convinced that at least a few could find this intellectually and spiritually constructive by the way I look at things based in my fortunate experience.

I also have seen how my brain, my cold intelligence, struggles to the limit of its capacity when it is challenged in dealing with another nonmaterial reality and the concept of God, as is the case when I go back to rethink my experience of my death and all its amazing significance. It is when my brain reaches its limits. It could well be described as a brain bending task, but then that is the moment I engage my mind to be in charge of the most wonderful challenge that my intellect can have. It is when the process of consciousness takes place with my mind in control of the interpretation of such reality.

From all I have said above, and I will expand in other chapters of this book, the elements that surface in the process of death as I experienced it all touch on the three pillars of human knowledge: religion, philosophy and science. Therefore, I humbly want to share my thoughts with members of those disciplines who could be interested in my views in hopes they will find them of value in their fields.

It is not that I want to pretend to have a revelation or a message of a religious nature or that I have been chosen to enlighten humankind as I said in the previous chapter. After all, the authentic different faiths of the world have always responded to the needs of humankind in finding the ultimate truth.

But having gathered all this empirical information in what could be described as a "glitch" in the process of my death I believe it can provide a valuable perspective that can confirm and substantiate many of the findings of human knowledge that coalesce in giving us from our material reality the image of the Creator. The same testimony could open a larger window in the personal lives of those progressive individuals who are seeking to develop an expanded image of God.

*"There is an orderliness in the universe, there is an unal-
terable law governing everything and every being that exists or
lives. It is no blinding law; for no blinding law can govern the
conduct of living beings."*

- Mohandas Gandhi

CHAPTER 5

MY EXPERIENCE IN THE PROCESS OF DEATH AND THE UNIVERSE

There are many brilliant and respected minds in the field of astrophysics who are making tremendous advances in the knowledge of the universe. Most impressive are the latest findings made with the use of the amazing technology of space telescopes like the Hubble, the X-ray Chandra, the Spitzer, and the new generation of gigantic telescopes being built on earth enhanced with the most powerful computers available these days and the use of Laser Corrected Telescope Optics to overcome the distortions of the earth atmosphere.

Those findings can be witnessed by anyone, in any corner of the world, who has a computer connected to the internet. They are not exclusive for the use of scientists. All we have to do is go

37

to Google® or Yahoo® and enter one of the most popular sites of NASA or HUBBLE to enjoy all those stunning pictures of stars, galaxies, nebulas, clusters, etc.

HDTV is also providing the same visual information of those important discoveries through the popular program, The Discovery Channel, and many others at one's disposal. But in this case, with the use of computer programs, those images are blended with science, visual art and lots of fantastic imagination, to make us feel in virtual reality. We can navigate through space and visit the celestial objects displayed without having to leave our rooms.

It is evident that cosmology has advanced a long way since the rudimentary telescope made by Galileo Galilei in the 16th century which expanded the eyes of mankind to see the real scale and mechanics of the universe. These days, with the new powerful telescopes in the hands of science, we can reach to the edge of the cosmos at a distance of 13.7 billion light years.

However, these spectacular discoveries made by science are still short of responding to the most basic and fundamental questions about the creation of the universe. The apparent reason seems to be that the scope of this field of knowledge has been determined with a self limited parameter that dismisses the causation of the universe based on "the principle of economy," which states that when science cannot explain something it does not deal with it at all. It sounds absurd but some of the most renowned cosmologists actually use this justification. However, the evident reason that they cannot hide is that the old materialistic approach of science to explain the origin of the physical reality of the universe is insufficient.

Fortunately there are some other cosmologists in growing numbers who have an authentic curiosity and honest desire to know and understand our reality in profundity. They are the progressive men and women of science ready to reach to the heart of the matter to understand and make sense of the whole body of evidence in a display of real scientific integrity. Not satisfied in only looking at the surface, they are open to accept a more suitable and honest form of reasoning to reach the truth about the creation of the universe and to make sense of this wonder of nature.

Notwithstanding the above, here is succinctly what science can tell us so far about the Big Bang: From nothingness the reality of space-time and the basic forces that shape and govern the functioning of the universe came to exist from an infinitely large amount of energy, condensed in an infinitely small point, at an infinitely high temperature. From here mass, the stuff of matter, started to come into reality in the first billions of a second when the tremendous temperatures descended. First, as a soup of plasma made of quarks, gluons, electrons and a combination of other particles called hadrons. Ten microseconds later some of those particles became agglutinated by the action of the basic forces into protons and neutrons (the stuff that makes the nucleus of the atoms). When the temperature descended to ten million degrees the phase of that plasma state, was transformed into atoms of hydrogen, helium, and lithium, with their electrons surrounding the nucleus, a phenomena which is called a "phase transition."

That basic condition remained for three hundred thousand years with the space of the universe expanding at an incredibly high speed (much faster than the speed of light), and with light being created by the interactions of those atoms producing photons (as in turning a switch on). Before that, total darkness prevailed in the first phase of the universe.

From here, the process of the creation of the first stars and galaxies took place later produced by the workings of the sculpturing force of gravity that condensed the existing atoms into these celestial objects. But eventually, a few billions of years later, new more complex atoms like oxygen and carbon (the essential blocks of biological life, together with hydrogen produced before) were made by the powerful super nova explosions of the first collapsing stars. The process of life in the universe we inhabit today began to take shape.

Using all that knowledge cosmologists tell us that the universe and its components, matter, space-time, electromagnetic forces, the weak and the strong forces, gravity and temperature, all were formed with the Big Bang from an infinitely dense concentration of energy in a point infinitely small. However science doesn't know or care about where this energy came from.

I want to make reference to this fundamental piece of knowledge in relation to my experience in the process of my death despite that such experience could be labeled by some just a mystical phenomenon. Being well aware of the materialistic approach of science I can see also that the hard core members of the scientific community will raise objections to the relationship of my findings with the explanation of the universe.

Nevertheless, because I find an incredible coincidence between the scientific significance of the Big Bang and my own experience I think it is worth of telling. I am sure that on the other hand the progressive scientists mentioned above who try to make sense of the universe with their open minds will find this novel perspective especially interesting.

In the process of my death when I remained suspended in that void of emptiness the state of nothingness that I described before was also transformed into a new phase at the moment I encountered that extremely little particle containing a tremendous concentration of energy, of living energy, that resulted in the expression of the infinite power of God. Such transformational phenomenon in the process of my death which brought me into a new reality of life from such state of darkness actually corresponds one hundred percent to a phase transition like the one that took place in the birth of the universe as described by modern cosmology: from the nothing, an infinitely enormous concentration of energy gives place to the creation of physical reality with the universe.

The unambiguous conclusion is that the universe and humankind follow a similar process, the same pattern, to reach our ultimate reality. Of course it had to be that way. Both realities, the material reality of the universe and our new reality we find through death are created by the same Architect!

41

It is fascinating to see the coincidences and parallels between these two dimensions of reality and how they come into being. Both come from the "nothing" and came into being through the infinite energy of God. Shouldn't this tell us something about the stubborn denial of hard core science to accept the intervention of a Creator of the universe?

It is important for me to say that at the time I went through my process of death I was not aware of the scientific description of the Big Bang for the simple reason that the theory had just been formulated but not confirmed by the findings of the Cosmic Microwave Background Radiation which took place in 1964. Furthermore, most of the members of the astrophysicist community were not fully convinced of it until the 1990s when they found new evidences of such occurrence. Some years later I learned of the scientific findings of the Big Bang and was able to see the correlation of both events.

But the birth of the universe is not the only fact that tells us of a Creator. In my view the Big Bang is also correlated with another fact of amazing significance, the anthropic structure of the universe which is a solid scientific fact. What this involves is nothing less than the purposely intelligent design of the cosmos to have the precise elements and conditions necessary to produce and sustain, first step by step, and then by leap and bounds, the biological life of humans.

In another chapter I will go into more detail about several of those well known factors, in order to describe this particular characteristic of our universe. In short, I can say now that according to solid scientific data, we would not be here if only one of those factors were out of tune with minuscule variations. In other words, it seems like the universe was expecting us to come into reality at an exact time and its precise configuration is evidence that the universe was custom made precisely to fit the presence of the Children of God!

Each of these two factors, the birth of the universe and its anthropic configuration, tell us unambiguously, and without any doubt, about the participation of a Creator of the universe. The Same One I encountered in my amazing journey through the process of my death. But more abundantly, the intimate relationship of one factor with the other takes us to conclude what science should conclude by itself. The linking of one factor with the other shows that there is a cause and an effect in the universe. The cause is God and the effect is us, humankind.

If the above amazing scientific facts made available to anyone are not convincing the only inescapable outcome left for the skeptics will be the unstoppable ticking of the clock when their own time takes them to touch the face of God. The only hope left is that when getting to that point those individuals do not persist in maintaining their self-centered unwillingness to accept God because that could mean their instantaneous destination to the place with no God, the nothingness!

To conclude and connecting again with what I experienced in my death, I can also see that as intelligent design produced the universe, which sustains our material biological life while we are in this world, something similar takes place but in another direction in the process of our deaths. Coming into the reality of the universe in the process of our births we get our material body, our material reality. Going out of this world through the process of our deaths we leave our biological bodies to become another kind of entities. This is because the only way we are going to have the necessary conditions to meet face to face with our Father in full view, in His own dimension, will be when we get rid of our material bodies and our consciousness expands to a new level so we can acquire the new kind of body suitable to merge with the essence of God.

But the cleansing process of our deaths with its different stages has been designed by God in a similar process in His creation of the universe to adapt us to such form of existence. So our complete reality, first the universe where we come into physical reality, and then the new reality we encounter in our deaths, is the striking evidence of the same hand in its making.

"If you want to turn your life around, try thankfulness. It will change your life mightily."

- Gerald Good

CHAPTER 6

The Impact this Experience Had on My Life

From the first moment of my return to this world after my humbling experience with death, I realized that my perception of life was totally changed having found how our reality in this world and my human dimension makes sense only when centered in the Truth of this wonderful Being that I encountered in my journey to the other world.

In this process of personal growth I was touched from head to toe and among other things I learned to better appreciate God's creation, beginning with what we have in our treasured planet. The most obvious change was my capacity to value more and appreciate what we normally have at our disposal on an everyday basis and we tend to take for granted, starting with the simple but important fact that we can breath because evidently God has provided us with all the precious air we could need.

The way my throat closed completely as a result of a catastrophic allergic reaction totally preventing me from breathing for several minutes could be considered one of most horrible ways of dying.

On average, a normal person breaths seventeen times every minute, approximately twenty five thousand times in a day. As an automatic action we don't think about it, but if we stop breathing for more than sixty seconds then we really pay attention to it and start to experience a terrible pain and desperation.

After the experience I went through, air is not a given thing anymore. I became obsessed with clean air. I value air more than gold and maybe for the same reason I have learned to enjoy and appreciate very intensely other accessory qualities like its purity, its warmth, and additionally the aromas of nature mixed in the air like the clean air in the mountains, the deserts and the oceans, the aroma of mowed grass, etc.

One of my greatest pleasures is to walk outdoors breathing slowly and very deeply and trying to identify the many different plants and trees by the aromas they produce. My dream that I would like to accomplish one of this days is to be able to take a trip by road all the way from Mexico to Alaska accompanied by a big German Shepherd dog, camping along the road any time I find a good spot. I can see myself walking and enjoying the clean air in the desert of the Baja California Peninsula, on the beaches of California and the Canadian forests, until reaching Mount McKinley in Alaska. That is my next big project after I publish this book, but I am still trying to convince my wife to come with me.

As my old professor of History of Economics at the university taught me, if air were scarce imagine how much we would be willing to pay for it. Obviously in that situation we would pay more for air than for gasoline or even food for the simple reason that without the vital air we would not survive a few minutes. You just ask me!

But also, thanks to well known Dr. Andrew Weil and his teachings on preventive medicine from the perspective of the intimate connection of body and mind, I have learned how important is to know how to breath right. At different times of the day in accordance with my needs to focus better when I do exercise or relax when prepared to go to sleep and rest better, I use his breathing techniques with wonderful results in my well-being.

A more significant impact of my experience with death has been to develop a concern for the ecology before it became popular as it is today. With that kind of sensitivity it became very difficult for me to continue living in Mexico City. Mexico City had ironically been named by the Spaniard conqueror Hernan Cortez the most pristine city in the world, but with its out of control growth, it became one of the most polluted cities in the planet where on too many occasions people cannot even see the beautiful mountains surrounding the city and on some very bad days not even the buildings across the street. So I always wanted to leave that crowded metropolis and fortunately I was able to convince my parents and the rest of my family to go back to the city of Zacatecas from where we came originally. That town is still an untouched paradise, a small beautiful colonial city with the clearest blue skies and purest air in the whole country. I love that place!

Afterwards I became more and more concerned with air quality because I am seeing, as many others do, how the extent of the pollution on our precious planet earth is mainly caused by the carbon dioxide released in the atmosphere by the increasing number of gas guzzler cars and the coal plants to produce electricity. In my view these actions clearly respond to the insatiable economic interests of the big oil groups which profit with total disregard of a sustainable ecology. But I am also convinced that at the same time it reflects a much deeper struggle, a struggle that unveils the forces of evil behind this immoral ideology of our days.

These two single polluting sources of energy together are producing a devastating effect not only on the quality of the air we breathe but also in terms of a climate change which is affecting the whole ecology of our planet because of the intricate interconnection of the elements of nature.

But that is not the only cause of the ecological degradation. The way society has been dragged so far by these immoral forces with the promotion of a mentality of unlimited consumerism adds to the destruction of the environment, driving people to buy in excess, consume in excess, produce trash in excess, build bigger houses, make bigger cars, etc. All is linked to the same struggle directed to the destruction of the pristine and unique environment God made for us. But in the last instance such struggle is directed to the disruption of the harmony between men and nature, with the first evident results in the increasing pandemic problems like obesity and autism and its myriad consequences in the whole health and unhappiness of the individual.

If we look back in time only a few years we can see how the mentality of unlimited consumerism and waste of resources has already resulted in a terrible damage to our beautiful planet, a unique place in the universe that has all the necessary conditions to incubate and sustain our precious life. It looks as if humanity is losing the struggle in view of the tremendous damage done to the ecology of our planet with repercussions in the way modern society has to live in a degraded environment.

I don't pretend to have the qualities of a moralist but sometimes I sincerely wonder if we all have the necessary moral and intellectual capacity not only to appreciate and value our gifts in this world, but also to stand up to those forces of evil that would wish the destruction of humankind. For the same reason I think that God wants to see if we, His creation can rise to the challenge of responding with courage, intelligence and responsibility to take care of our natural environment with the freedom to act that we have received from Him.

However there is good news. These days we are beginning to see a growing number of people keenly aware of the problem, especially the brave younger generations who are becoming involved in a world wide movement to save our planet. There is hope after all that good and moral behavior can prevail over those blind people who with their irresponsible actions produce damage to our environment, becoming instruments of the forces of destruction!

Obviously another great change I have experienced has been how much I value now the opportunity of life which has given to me the opportunity to show my thanks to God.

In consequence, I am trying to make use of every single minute of my life entirely focused in pursuing that purpose, and trying not to get distracted or waste any time. Because of my experience with death I am perfectly aware of the fragility of our material life and how fast time passes. It does not matter how young or strong we are, as I was when I had my previous encounter with death. At that time I felt like I was indestructible.

When the time comes, and usually comes unexpectedly, we just go. So, having this in mind I am trying to be ready for the next time, which could be just around the corner.

As I have said before, my experience with death has confirmed for me the truth about our Father, which has helped me in appreciating His creation of the universe integrated in nature and humans, which I see as a measure of His infinite love for us.

My natural sense of curiosity about nature, the universe and humanity, has been expanded exponentially due to the very humbling motivation I received with my enlightening experience. With that perspective in mind I literally devour any piece of information that falls in my hands about those subjects. I even have plans if death does not come for me before, to go back to the university so I can go deeper in the study of some of those subjects, in particular research in epistemology, philosophy, psychology and physics.

As a logical consequence of the above I honestly can say that I don' t know what it means to be bored, not even for one minute. In many occasions I hear people around me say they are bored, especially people who live the good life in the high society. To me it is proof that focusing only with the material lenses of life takes us to see only empty panaceas. Life is extremely fascinating and beautiful when its fundamental focus is God!

My interest in epistemology is to be able to understand better the process of reasoning in our mental efforts to gain knowledge. I am convinced that to a great extent the problems encountered in the history of mankind in understanding the fundamental questions in the different areas that deal with reality (physical, philosophical, psychological, and theological). All have a common basis in the methodology of reason which has not reached its main conclusions despite all the efforts by the best minds engaged in this fundamental endeavor through the history of philosophy.

I also would like to dig deeper into the study of ethics and moral values to see how and in what situations these elements that make us humans should necessarily be integrated with the different methods of reason. All these concerns come to me because in too many cases the processes of using only cold reasoning in knowledge without any reference to morality and ethics have taken us in an opposite direction in finding what is good for mankind. And if that weren't enough, that limited approach of empty reasoning has created mental obstacles for the acceptance of a Creator which limits the understanding of our reality and obscures the road to our ultimate destiny.

Complementing all of the all the above, I am also interested in the study of the brain from the angle of psychology in conjunction with metaphysics and theology so I can understand with more precision the interrelation of our brains with our minds.

I am interested in physics because I am fascinated with the amazing coincidences between the elements and phases that I encountered in the process of my death and what is going on with many of the natural phenomena in our material life such as the causes and birth of the universe and the phases it went through in its evolution until reaching its present condition.

Something fascinating and of great significance that we can learn from the universe is the fact that of its anthropic structure which has been scientifically observed and corroborated in so many of its structural characteristics, confirms that the universe has been tailored in precise detail to have Man. The evidence behind this amazing truth is that the universe has a cause and a purpose and it is related to the presence of humans in it!

But this way of thinking should not limit our focus to us alone in this particular earth. These days science is beginning to look for the possibility of life in other worlds aiming their most powerful telescopes to the stars which could have their own orbiting planets similar to our planet earth. Just imagine the potential number of civilizations, not just biological life that can be encountered in the whole universe if we consider that our galaxy can have at least one civilization, humankind. Having accounted our cosmologists so far one hundred billion galaxies in the universe the minimum reasonable number of civilizations could very well coincide with such enormous number of galaxies, one hundred billion, at least one per galaxy!

If we are willing to accept an Intelligence reflected in the consequent anthropic design of the whole universe, our minds should also expand with all the implications of such reasonable possibilities to be well prepared for the inescapable encounter in the future with our brothers from other regions of the universe. A new way of thinking about the universe and the meaning of life in its immensity should wake us up to the fact that we are not alone and that the concept of the human race is larger and more complex than what we have been thinking. With the strong possibility of interacting with other civilizations in other parts of the universe an emergent concept of a universal race is in our future.

That is why I would like to go deeper into these and other aspects of science to make a better connection of these facts of nature with what I found in my own experience, but taking into account at all times the reality of humans and our transcendental purpose.

Before I had my experience with death, maybe because of my young age mixed with my thirst for adrenalin and a strong inclination for adventure, driving at high speeds, swimming in the open ocean with sharks, never refusing a good fight, etc., I could say that I showed a total disdain for my life.

Furthermore, I thought that acting as if death could never reach me was a good reason for people to admire me. The combination of that and my macho image of myself thanks to my Mexican background, gave me a strong incentive for doing very dangerous things. The number of broken bones in my body give an account of those restless times with my nose broken two times, my left arm, ribs, my right hand, and several fingers. Now however, remembering those times, I see myself not only as ridiculous but very irresponsible.

Having been so close to leaving this world for good made me make a turn of one hundred and eighty degrees. No more irresponsible actions. On the contrary, now I am so careful that sometimes I am even criticized for being too cautious in everything I do. I have had a taste of the extremes in life!

This transformation includes my interest in maintaining good health, especially through good nutrition and exercise. What is clear to me is that now I am aware of the importance of taking better care of myself including my physical health so I can respond to my enormous responsibility of maintaining a functional body. The fact that I am married to a good nutritionist has definitely helped a lot. Now I contemplate my life with my body and my health together as a precious gift that I must keep in the best condition possible until I am called back to my final destiny waiting for me.

Today I could say that still I am not afraid of dying, but for very different reasons. To me facing death now is not just for the thrill and the adrenaline or for an ego reason that does not make any sense at all. I am patiently waiting death to come with no fear at all because I leave it in the hands of God. He will be the

One to decide when and how I should start my journey to reach Him. It can be today, tomorrow or take a few more years. All I want is to make sure that I am going to be ready for the moment of truth whenever it comes again.

That is why I frequently have the feeling as if I were in an airport, with my ticket in hand just waiting to be called for my departure. But I remain tranquil without any fears, because with my faith reinforced by my wonderful experience in my previous journey, I know that I will be taking the best aircraft with the best pilot to get me safely to my final destination!

Something else that I achieved with my humble experience in dying and encountering my Creator, has been the comforting feeling of the very special friendship I made with Him. I recognized immediately and without any doubt that the wonderful being I was meeting at that moment was My Creator, my celestial Father, an entity of pure and great energy made of love, intelligence and harmony.

Obviously the overpowering image and the dimension that a Being of such magnitude and magnificence represents makes us elicit our greatest respect and admiration, besides of our own love and gratitude for everything He is giving to us, beginning with our existence.

As I mentioned before, in the last stage of the process of my death I had a very clear consciousness of the tremendous force pulling me towards such source and how I was beginning to be absorbed in his own essence. But I was aware of something more, His own happiness in having me. It was His love and joy that I felt from Him, it was the fabulous encounter of the Father with his son.

But after my return to this world, having asked Him to grant me one more minute of this life to have the opportunity of showing my gratitude, I have kept my communication with God on an everyday basis because I feel that while He is waiting for me to go back one of these days, at the same time wants to know everything about me, and has established a way to communicate through my Mind, as He does with everybody else. All we have to do is to express our own will and sincere desire to maintain open the line of communication that connects with Him for that purpose.

God will be there always at the other end of the line waiting to listen from us like a Father, but also as a friend wanting to hear every intimate detail of our lives, of our moments of joy and success in our lives, but also of our moments of doubts and worries, even the many little things that make up our days but we hesitate in sharing with others.

This is why I believe that having the right conception of God as our Creator I am allowed to humbly enjoy Him also as a close and very special friend. Something similar happens when we talk to our worldly parents. We talk to them with all our respect about everything of interest, however there are many instances when we need to share in a more intimate way some things that will bring us closer to them.

In my practical life I also try to apply this approach but directed to my own children. I am their father and of course I interact with them in that role, however with the desire to have a fluid and constant communication with both of them, most of the times we talk as friends do (by cellular phone these days because they live far away) about the little things revolving around our lives. That happens with my son, Ricardo, who just called recently to tell me how proud he was because he was able to make the wire connection to his computer with a projector he received as a present from one of his friends. It is the same with my daughter Ana Cristina. She especially likes to share how she is doing with her classes and what she is cooking for dinner. The idea is to have the joy of talking to each other as friends and to keep our lines of communication open.

Having a vision of my connection at that level of intimacy with God motivates me to share everything I find of significance with Him, but especially the good things. I know that as a good friend he offers us his shoulder to listen to us in our bad moments, as it was the day of the 9/11 when thousands of innocent people died and I was struck, as everybody else, with the terribly bad news. However, I am more inclined to share with Him instead the good news because I know that He want us to be happy and not sad. I am certain that this is His purpose with our creation.

So with that perspective in mind, anyone could understand the great motivation I have in my purpose to conform my life in a positive frame trying to make Him happy with my own scale of happiness. This vision of connecting with God also helps me a great deal in the surroundings in which I live (including with my own family) because that kind of attitude reflects our positive image in the eyes of people around us, which, as I have seen, helps a lot in promoting a positive atmosphere wherever we go. This is also the way I can identify and connect right away with other people who also live with this vision in their own lives.

This kind of attitude has been also of great help to me when no matter what, I still face real problems that I cannot avoid. I have seen in several occasions when I have been in the middle of a big problem that does not seem to have a solution, if I face it with this positive attitude, usually I find the solution. It is because this way we attract the light that transforms darkness!

"We need to find God, and He cannot be found in noise and restlessness. God is the friend of silence. See how nature -- trees, flowers, grass, -- grows in silence; see the stars, the moon and the sun, how they move in silence... We need silence to be able to touch the souls."

- Mother Teresa

CHAPTER 7

MY NEED TO COMMUNICATE WITH GOD ALL THE TIME

Since my close encounter with death which allowed me to face my Creator I have a very strong spiritual need to find a way of maintaining my communication with Him. This need could be similar to the practice in the different religions of praying.

Many people pray to God in the particular framework of their religion, but many others do it in their individuality for adapting better to their personal needs in the way they can see God. But in this purpose I think there is no difference how we do it as long as we feel this need and we are convinced that our Creator is also inclined to listen to us.

As a child raised in the religion of my parents, I was taught how to pray in a formal way. However my experience with death which gave me the very special opportunity of facing my Creator so I could reach a precise and complete awareness of His image, made me want to find a way to keep a permanent connection and communication with God all the time that responds to my new particular needs.

But I still value very highly praying in groups any time I go to my old church or I am invited to other churches. Praying together with many as one, I think, should also convey a special message to God because we make evident that we can tune our elevated feelings to our celestial Father in harmony, as brothers and sisters united by the same purpose. I believe that this is one of the highest manifestations of the real essence of the children of God, praying in concert with others, in harmony with the universe!

Nevertheless, I still have the need to communicate at the personal level. This does not mean that I consider myself having a better way of praying nor that I pretend to make of it an example to follow by others. Moreover, in this regard I feel that I can learn from others. My wish is only to point to my real and permanent need of thanking God for all the blessings I receive from Him, and my joy of communicating and sharing my feelings (especially happy ones) and thoughts of value (especially positive ones) that can come to me in my everyday life.

My way is very simple and is mainly in those quiet moments of the early morning when I can concentrate better before turning on the news and being driven by the beat of the busy days.

Not pretending to reach a level of meditation or to look for a revelation only to be able to reach the calm and peace that comes to me with the sole idea of God. I sit down in the living room for a few moments (usually with a good cup of hot tea in my hands) to give thanks for another day of life in this world and my family. My purpose is not directed in asking anything. It is to show my gratitude to our Father for everything. After all this is the reason that brought me back to this world. I only have asked God' s help in those very critical occasions when I face situations out of my hands to resolve, as can be a delicate health problem of someone close to me or a world wide crisis.

In that tranquil atmosphere I also reiterate my will to continue using the time granted with my second opportunity and I try to foresee the moment of my final departure so I do not lose sight of my purpose. However I use the moment to also enjoy God and try to convey to Him my happiness for living and for this world of His creation with all my loved ones and the wonders of nature. I know that if I can perceive the light of the morning and the singing of the birds I am capturing the reflection of His beautiful image which is all around us imbedded in nature.

I have to recognize that before I get engaged in my normal activities, I wonder sometimes what kind of day I will have ahead of me considering that we are living very convulsed times (that's why sometimes I hesitate to turn on the daily news), but the answer I find is always the same. Having started the day with God in my mind and knowing that he watches us all the time from Heaven I gain strength and confidence that I am going to be able to face any challenges that could arise and   continue with my life and my purpose.

Once my activities develop as the day goes by I always try to find at least a spare minute to share my thoughts with God, in particular when I learn something new of special interest, or meet outstanding people who impress me for the high quality of their human values who direct their beautiful actions to people in need. Fortunately we have many of these people arising in these days of economic difficulties and we have to recognize the good job of the media that brings them to the surface. As I live in a beautiful city surrounded by majestic mountains that I enjoy so much I can also share these feelings of joy with my Creator.

In certain situations when I am concentrating on something of value or interest I make my comments to God but obviously not anticipating or necessarily demanding a direct and verbal response from Him. I am perfectly aware from my experience with death when I reached Him that He is in His own particular dimension which is not the same as where we live now so He is not materially present with us and neither, properly speaking, He does talk to us with sounds because of His particular substance. He does it through our mind and His own Mind connecting and communicating with us all the time but there are also many other rich and diverse ways we can feel His presence.

I was driving home on 9/11 after work in Los Angeles on Highway 101 towards Woodland Hills feeling, as everybody else, profound sadness for the tragic death of more than three thousand people who died instantly when the twin towers collapsed in New York and I had watched in shock that morning on live TV.

In front of me at that precise moment the sun was setting in a splendorous fashion leaving only the half portion of the sun visible beyond the rounded mountains. The intense blue skies were completely clear and there was only one elongated cloud made of many little bright dots that extended from one extreme from the south east and the other to the west exactly to the point where the sun was setting at that moment so you can imagine the brightness and the beautiful color of the cloud. In the first instance the view impressed me for its special beauty but a few moments later and thinking about the coincidence with the tremendous tragedy of that day a chilling feeling struck me. It looked to me as if I was seeing those thousands of innocent people who had been killed by the terrorist acts waiting in line to be welcomed by God!

I am sure that I could be labeled a sentimentalist but if we are convinced of God then we also can see in many ways how His image is reflected in our world, from the tiny things to the breathtaking vastness of the universe, but also in giving meaning and making sense of our life. All that is required from us, is to have the will to talk to Him and the disposition to keep our minds tuned to the right spiritual frequency.

At the end of the day just when I am going to bed making a balance of what I accomplished I ask myself if I did something good, if I learned something new, if I was able to laugh, but mainly if I did not hurt the feelings or the dignity of anyone. If at least this is what I accomplished of the day then I can offer it to God!

PART TWO

A FUNDAMENTAL REFERENCE IN OUR HUMAN DIMENSION

"You are a primary existence. You are a distinct portion of the essence of God, and contain a certain part of Him in yourself. Why then are you ignorant of your noble birth? You carry a God about within you, poor wretch, and know nothing of it."

- Epictetus

"Without God, what would we do to make sense of our ephemeral existence in this world?"

— Unknown Author

CHAPTER 8

A World with No God?

It is widely known these days, some intellectuals and academicians, reach the conclusion that God does not exist by explaining the universe in its complexity and laws that govern it, including humans, and everything else that makes our reality, as a simple product of "chance", a mathematical chance. A simplistic and short sighted approach that dismisses our Creator.

Scientific thought as it is employed in our days began in the Middle Ages as a reaction against the authority of the church. However the new approach to explain reality went to the extreme in rejecting the concept of God and his role as the creator of our reality and the universe. The undeniable and horrendous abuses made in those times by some churches in Europe using distorted conceptions of God to gain power from their participation in the political arena and corruptly supporting the monarchy of their time, naturally produced a reaction against faith replacing it with a new ideology, pure reason and materialism.

All this, no doubt, produced progress for society at that moment of history in the liberating movement of the individual, opening the gates at the same time to the extraordinary advancement of science and technology. However, this pendular movement, as usually happens in this kind of social reactions, went too far in giving birth to a mentality in the science world of rejecting the idea of God based on a supposedly scientific approach. These days the rejection of God is like a fashionable credential required to enter the club of the scientific elite.

Unfortunately, such attitude builds again a new obstacle to the right conception of the individual. We tried to resolve the gross distortions of the past dark ages with its wicked obscurantism, superstition and repression, but now with the extreme reaction of the scientific and intellectual community we are being dragged to a new narrow and distorting materialist mentality.

Because the excessive emphasis in the objective knowledge over the subjective and the prevalence of cold reason over intuition, the resulting description of humans is just as biological entities made by pure chance. With the use of statistics and mathematics and the use of supercomputers the so called social sciences pretend to predict human behavior, predict the destiny of humankind. With this cold mentality scientists are more and more inclined to wrongly see humans as computers with artificial intelligence. However the simple truth is that they still cannot even explain how humans can achieve consciousness.

This, in my view, is an attack to our capacity to see ourselves integrated with the elements that make us as real humans. Such distortion would be the equivalent to build a mental barrier to the acceptance of our consciousness as our highest expression of human intelligence that connects us with a higher Intelligence. We cannot close our eyes to the rich and complex reality that defines us as humans with God at the center of our world.

If the scientific community honestly wants to help humanity, it should revise its methodology in their field of knowledge to allow the consideration not only of the material elements that constitute our universe, but including the undeniable causes of the cosmos originating in the dimension of our Creator. In other words, if they really want to be able to understand the universe, the concept of God will have to be included. There cannot be the world without God!

Not making this adjustment eliminates the possibility of reaching valid conclusions in regard to the many holes and half truths in their own realm of knowledge, which ironically surface as there are more discoveries in science and technology. What is dark energy? What is dark matter? These are only two of the many basic pieces of the puzzle for science still unresolved, despite that they are unmistakably detected in the accelerated expansion of the universe and the rotational speed of stars in the galaxies. But these fundamental elements that conform the observable universe are beyond the reach of the skeptical scientists. Furthermore, they probably will never be able to explain them if they do not open their narrow scope to accept the transcendental nature of our physical world.

And at a more fundamental level, what is energy and its source? How do the laws of nature carry their instructions to conform the universe with its anthropic structure tailored to the exact measure of man? The fact is that I could continue with the list on and on. All these are fundamental factors in the conception of the universe but science these days only juggles with them with the most elaborate and exotic hypothesis that come closer to a world of fantasy and magic than to reality!

The hand of God in the creation of the universe is in front of us in plain sight everywhere we look and can't be denied, so to try to find the secrets of the cosmos without any links with its real causation not only would close the door to unveiling the truth, but would be an ironic contradiction that could take humankind back to the dark ages. But this time the ghosts of the old dark ages would be replaced with real cyber monsters. Life without God in the scope to comprehend our world would make no sense and humankind would get lost in the darkness for ever.

"The idea of death, the fear of it, haunts the human animal like nothing else; it is a main string of human activity -- designed largely to avoid the fatality of death, to overcome it by denying in some way it is the final destiny of man."

- Ernest Becker

C H A P T E R   9

The Meaning of Death

We usually depict death with the frightful figure of a skull resting over cross bones. It is so graphic that it has been used on the flags of the pirates to produce fear to their poor victims, Halloween, or for other purposes like warnings for poison, electrocution, etc.

The image of the skull is further complemented with a black background that reinforces the idea of death. In many cultures widows dress totally in black. Of course, the idea we associate with the word death complemented with that figure and color is nothing else than the termination of life but with the unavoidable feeling of something fearful, sad, negative, bad, horrific, destructive. It is an idea that instinctively we want to avoid for the unpleasant sentiment of terror that conveys.

From beginning to end in the history of humankind the concept of death has been reflected in many of its chapters as a constant factor in its making. The Egyptian civilization organized its whole culture, the architecture of the cities and social organization around their dead, especially the dead monarchs. Many of the great pyramids built by those milenary civilizations are material proof of this mentality.

In Mexico, the Day of the Dead which takes place every November 2nd, is one of the most important traditions in the Mexican culture. It goes back as far as two thousand years. The indian civilizations believed that the spirit of the dead goes to heaven where it rests in peace but comes back to this world to be with their families for one day.

The tradition is that families (especially Indian families) go to the cemetery and spend the whole day at the tomb of their dead, taking food, mainly mole and tamales, and the drinks which the dead used to enjoy in life, usually tequila, mezcal, and pulque (all these three hard drinks are made of the fermentation of cactus juices). A special bread, "Pan de Muerto" is also made to offer to the dead as well as candy with the form of a skull made of sugar and highly decorated. These candy skulls end up being eaten by the children. People say that in eating that candy the Mexican children learn to see the light side of death.

In the homes, families set altars which are decorated with the same type of food and drinks, yellow flowers, candles, and pictures of the dead. These days all these rituals have mixed with the rituals of the Catholic church so the decoration of the altars is complemented with crosses and images of the Virgin of Guadalupe.

In the dark times of the Middle Ages the idea of death caused all kinds of fears impacting and distorting the minds of people. The fear of death became a powerful instrument of control and authority in the hands of unscrupulous rulers.

In modern times many despicable governments have used the threat of death on their own people to maintain their control. Not only as a threat but actually in committing atrocities and genocide such as in recent years in some Central American and South American countries as well as in some African countries.

Of course, in religion the idea of approaching death plays a central role and becomes the differentiating factor that determines the many branches of the religious expressions of humankind. Some churches have a more sinister conception of death but others look mostly at the positive meaning of death. For the occult, death is not so much related to the idea of the extinction of life but is used mainly to sustain the concept of fearful ghosts and evil spirits that come to earth to interact with humans.

Our feelings of the idea of death are imbedded in the deepest fibers of our biological nature as it is also with every other living creature on earth sharing with them what seems to be the strongest feeling we carry with us, the instinct of survival. In other words, the avoidance with all our strength and at any cost, of the termination of our life.

However, the feeling in humans is stronger than in animals

because not only do we carry it in our instinct but it is also reinforced with our human capacity of reasoning (we see others dying, so we know we are going to follow) and sentiments of solidarity and protection towards our peers and our loved ones. It is a trait that the animals don't seem to exhibit to this extent for their own except in the case of mothers with their cubs and some particular species like dolphins and elephants.

An animal cannot know in advance of his own doom until it faces in the very last moment the hungry teeth of a larger predator or the knife of the butcher. But in the case of some men the degree of pain and anguish with the pure idea of their inescapable future of death would explain all the desperate efforts in trying to avoid it, mostly by living in denial or getting numb to the idea. They emphasize in their minds the concept of the material world over the transcendental. This perception could explain the ulterior reason behind the growing number of skeptics being so terrified with death in the deepest caverns of their minds they try to close their eyes to the truth.

Many others, especially those with economic resources and a strong desire to maintain their self-centeredness forever, cling to the hopeful wish that the advances of modern medical technology will help them. They are willing to pay whatever they are asked for to get those resources for their advantage trying to desperately avoid falling in the arms of death.

Oscar Wilde, in his famous novel The Picture of Dorian Gray, makes a perfect description of the wicked mentality of those people who are willing to pay, even with their own souls, for their hedonistic wish of defeating death. These are the kind of mentalities that it could take for some individuals to run the tremendous risk of taking the road to the nothingness. The crucial moment when that could happen would be when facing their inescapable deaths, show their refusal to become merged with God because of their wish of not giving up their individuality, their self-love.

One of the imminent and most ominous dangers with the development of science without moral and ethical constraints is that it could be willing to respond to the desires to avoid death of those individuals. Several of the efforts in research and development in the fields of biotechnology, genetics, nanotechnology and informatics could be directed to develop mechanisms with the purpose to give immortality to some of them, or at least to extend their life spans so they can wait with the hope to achieve what they want in the future developments of science. Just imagine the terrible consequences of disrupting the balance of life on earth with the moral and social repercussions for humanity if these technological projects become a tangible reality.

With control over death man would gain power over the laws of nature but be ready for the unforeseeable consequences of challenging the powers of life and nature!

When I faced my own death, when my throat shut, I tried to remain calm preserving my macho dignity intact for a few moments. But after passing more than two minutes that apparent calm crumbled when reaching my limits of resisting without air. At that moment I felt that I had only a few remaining moments of life. Feeling a combination of pain with a tremendous anguish I realized that I was going to die.

The image of the cross that came to my mind as a token of my faith undoubtedly was of great moral support to me at that difficult moment when I was facing my final truth. A few moments later I was relieved of my unbearable physical pain and desperation thanks to the sudden disconnection of my body. But still at that new stage I was more convinced that I was dying so I was expecting that I could lose consciousness at any moment.

But it did not take place. On the contrary, my consciousness expanded as never before in life so with certain astonishment and relief I began to believe after all in the possibility of not being extinct and vanishing in the darkness forever. Then suddenly I was in another reality of total emptiness where there is not any light or sound not feeling at all the effects of gravity and no spatial or timely reference of any kind. That condition goes beyond the darkness. I was in a void where there was nothing except me as the only reality in that emptiness. I said to myself, "this is it, this is death. I am not vanishing but this is the other kind of death where I am in the nothing". Here I can be aware of my own death because I am here as the only reality!

However that situation, which from our perspective could be very frightening, remaining suspended in a void alone forever, did not scare me at the beginning. After all, I was very much aware that I did not cease to exist. I still was me with my full consciousness so I remained expectant. Because of my faith I was hopeful of a change of the unique situation despite I had not any clue of what could come next. But then in contrast, very vividly, I could feel there was something. A little particle of energy in that void that appeared from nowhere and immediately started to grow so I could perceive it like a small light that continued growing very rapidly. I was startled with curiosity for what it could be but immediately I answered myself, "Wait a minute. That is not a thing. It is a being of pure energy coming towards me really fast." I wondered who could be there with me. I came closer to that being because at the same time I was being pulled towards him. There was a moment when finally I exploded with joy and happiness. I was facing God!

Thanks to my fabulous experience, when I witnessed my own death, I can now interpret death in a very different way than before. The meaning of death to me now is life. Real life!

The idea of total extinction was overcome after the first stage of my death, when despite being disconnected from my body, I remained amazingly aware with my mind not only intact but even better. With an enhanced consciousness. At that point I knew for sure that I would not vanish. But the other conception of death that I encountered in the next stage where I landed in the nothing is very impressive but thank God not permanent. No, we don't vanish, but being there suspended in that void absolutely alone is not very appealing. But it serves to define the extreme and the contrast of what comes after, real and complete life with the presence of our Father!

It is very sad to think that some people could face death in the other terrible meaning of extinction or remaining suspended for ever in the nothingness. That could happen if driven by their wrong approach to death based in their misconceptions of our reality and blinded by their arrogance and feelings of self-centeredness and power. Those people cannot conceive their transcendence with God. Certainly such possibility would become a horrible way of dying.

However death in the sincere and complete acceptance of God is nothing else than an amazing path to life. We live to die and we die to live!

"We can understand almost anything, but we can't understand how we understand."

- Albert Einstein

CHAPTER 10

CONSCIOUSNESS

One of the greatest challenges for philosophy has been to complete the definition of what is the underlying principle for the level of conceptualization we need to attain in our minds to make sense of who we are and the reality that surrounds "consciousness". However up until now, and in spite of all the efforts by many brilliant people engaged in this endeavor, the results don't bring us a definite conclusion.

In modern times psychology has also taken the challenge attempting to identify it in our brains with a scientific approach making use of the most sophisticated advances in Magnetic Resonance Imaging. The latest efforts of this research in neuropsychology are beginning to expand to the field of quantum mechanics which implies that consciousness could take place beyond the enclosed area of the brain. It will be ironic if this new approach takes these prestigious researchers to where they should have started, in the realm of the soul. In the search for the last truth the road is often a circle.

I will try to make here a humble contribution to these efforts but for that purpose I simply will make use of the knowledge I gained from my experience with death, centered in the idea of God, which in my view is the essential piece of reference missing in the efforts mentioned above.

With this reference in sight, how can we define consciousness? In its first manifestation while we live in this world it is a capacity and a potential. This capacity is given by three elements bound together, our physical senses, our brain, and the soul. With the harmonic coalescing of these elements we develop the potential to reach human consciousness.

Coincidentally, what makes us humans is also the combination of these elements. This is because we share the same biological elements with the animals, including intelligence but we reach a higher level in our human dimension because God created us with a specific purpose in giving us a portion of His own essence. He is also the creator of all living forms in the universe but because he planted the seed of his own substance in us which is love we became human beings.

At the initiation of the process of death that I experienced (a transformational stage) I was able to perceive with all clarity these three elements that allow us consciousness as human beings while we are in this world. In the next stage of my journey I felt how I became detached from the baggage of my body leaving behind the physical senses and my brain while remaining

THE LIGHT AT THE END OF DARKNESS

very aware of myself. This phenomena could be compared to a rocket ship going up to orbit which at lift off from earth it starts with all the different components of the rocket but in the next stage as it gains height and speed it detaches from the main parts of its body and reaches orbit without that dead weight. It only keeps what is suitable for its journey to space.

In the beginning, with the information provided by my sensory organs, I began to be aware that I could die when I stopped breathing. Then my intelligence confirmed objectively the fact that I was dying when I went beyond the two minutes without air. But then what followed was a total disconnection with my body. At this point I realized very clearly that I was made up not only of my senses and my brain. Instead of losing consciousness it expanded to a higher level of clarity I had never experienced before which allowed me to be aware of what had remained of myself, my soul. I became aware with relief that in dying I was not ceasing to exist, but that I continued living in a different form.

Thanks to my experience with death I can see how consciousness has different levels of manifestation. First when we come to this world and develop the awareness of ourselves connecting this fact with the reality that surrounds us. At this point it is like an awakening. But it grows to a higher level, and becomes better established the more we think about our reality and let our innate essence lead us to conclude that we have been created by a superior entity when we finally find and accept God in our lives. At this point we reach human consciousness.

As it is mentioned in other chapters of this book, there are different ways for us to be aware of God while we remain in this world. The most natural and accessible is through faith and revelation with religion as the expression of both. Some saints call it divine inspiration. Also, we can reach that awareness through knowledge but only when produced by correct and honest reasoning accepting the moral element in us with the adoption of intuition. This would be the special intuition that many of the great thinkers of all times and even these days the progressive men of science must have been using to reach their particular concept of the Creator. Meditation, taken to its highest level, is another way of connecting with the Supreme Being.

The next level of consciousness, complete consciousness, is achieved when we die, when we make the journey to encounter God in all His love, intelligence and power, when becoming wrapped in absolute happiness we realize that we are going to be absorbed for eternity in His Substance! At this level our consciousness is already completely detached from our material state, remaining as the expression of our soul. Achieving this pure state it is enhanced reaching its full potential by the recognition of its ultimate essence which identifies with the essence of God.

As we can see in both levels of consciousness, human and total consciousness, there are two essential elements that interact to form the concept. On one side, it is us, our soul. On the other, it is our Creator. Without these two elements and without this interaction, which implies a connection, consciousness could not take place. In other words, all the searching and efforts to determine what is consciousness disregarding God, no matter the means, the approaches, and the brain power put to work in this endeavor, will never reach the ultimate conclusion!

Consciousness is not limited to our physical brain, it is not encased in our skull, it comes to be when our soul connects with our Creator. Moreover, this connection develops and grows stronger based on the interaction between our soul and God when we center our Father in our lives as our purpose! That's how we can feel His presence all the time despite the fact that He remains in His own realm, in His own dimension, while we remain in our material world.

I also believe that if I had died in the simple idea of death as a cessation of life, at that moment I should have lost my consciousness and just disappear into the nothingness from the face of earth forever. But none of that happened. On the contrary my consciousness became expanded and more acute than ever before allowing me to be completely aware of everything that was taking place. I was totally convinced that I was dying but not being turned off and at the same time I was amazed at the clarity of my awareness in every stage through my journey to my final destination. I witnessed my own death!

In different occasions I have learned about the opinion of some scientists, especially in the medical field, who try to explain in biochemical terms what they believe really happens. This approach always contradicts the validity of the claims of people about their near-death experiences with the detachment from their bodies. Their purpose is to try to use science to erode the basis of an explanation of consciousness linked to our souls.

They argue that when the brain detects the possibility of dying it produces huge amounts of opiates to cushion pain and anguish with all kinds of hallucinations. This would be the equivalent to what happens with drug addicts, but in this case the difference would be that the brain would be the provider of the drugs instead. Drug addicts would be very pleased to find out that they still can have drugs for free when they are dying, probably that's why there are so many suicides among them!

However, based on the most basic logic that doesn't sound like a solid argument. How is it that the brain, where the intelligence supposedly takes place, does exactly the opposite of making an intelligent decision when it simply could cease completely all brain activity to avoid every possibility of suffering?

These people say that the opiates produced by the brain at that critical moment are mainly to avoid pain and to produce a state of calm. However, from my own experience I can tell that the main form of suffering when we are dying does not come only from physical pain. The worst is when initially we become aware that we are dying and a tremendous fear and anguish comes to us at that moment in facing the idea of our imminent disappearance into the nothing.

That kind of fear is beyond the worst nightmare that we could have and whatever physical pain could come to us at that moment is nothing compared with that feeling of horror that any opiate could neutralize. Besides, as I described before about my experience, after a brief moment of intense pain initially suffered when I could not breath any air into my lungs. I felt very clearly a sudden and total disconnection with my body including my brain and consequently could not feel anything any more. In that condition how is it that if I do not feel my body at all the opiates are still performing their function making me aware of something, in which body?

Besides not making sense with logic, the scientific explanation is faulty because it is common knowledge that the brain is the most susceptible of all our organs to suffer irreversible damage in only a few minutes, in most cases after six minutes, due to lack of oxygen when other organs can survive between fifteen or twenty minutes without the precious element. How is it that the brain keeps functioning in high gear exhausting its last reserves of energy producing huge amounts of opiates when its neurons are just struggling to maintain life without the indispensable oxygen?

Finally, how is it that the neurons which are dying due to the lack of oxygen can produce at that difficult moment a level of awareness as never before when they had available all the oxygen they needed to function normally?

If a materialistic science wants to erode the basis of the transcendental explanation of the phenomena of consciousness it will have to look to other approaches with better arguments.

"Is the system going to flatten you out and deny your humanity, or are you going to be able to make use of the system to the attainment of human purposes?"

- Joseph Campbell

CHAPTER 11

THE OBSTACLES TO REACH HAPPINESS IN THIS WORLD

After having lived in Sonora for one year, where my father had no luck in his search for silver and gold in the mines, and running out of money, we returned in 1948 to Zacatecas, our home town, and came to live for a while at my grandparent's home, my mother's parents. At that time I was four years old and my father was broke (in his life he went into bankruptcy several times while relentlessly searching for silver and gold in the mines). I recall very vividly that time as one of my most treasured memories for the rich and happy life I was lucky to live in those far away times.

The city of Zacatecas was a little mining town founded by the Spanish conquerors in the year 1546. Having discovered some of the richest mines in the world in those years they had plenty of money to spend on the colonial town nested under a beautiful mountain with three symmetrical peaks called "La Bufa." UNESCO has given the city the official designation of "Patrimony of Humanity" which requires the Mexican government to care for and preserve the colonial character of the city. Walking late at night in downtown when no cars on the road gives the sensation that time stood still there. One could feel transported back in time to the 1600s.

My grandparents' house was located on an oval street around "La Alameda." There was a big park with a very European flavor where every Saturday evening the Symphony Orchestra of the City of Zacatecas would play folklore and classical music for the enjoyment of the families gathered while all the children of the neighborhood, including me, played around and rode our bicycles into the night.

The old house was a big house with no gas or electric water heaters and not even chimneys, despite the city of Zacatecas being one the coldest places in the whole country. The thing about the house that made the biggest impression on me was the big corral where they had lots of chickens and pigs. Those were the times when people prepared most of their meals from scratch so the poor animals were there to be used for feeding the family (there were no supermarkets). I had the difficult experience of seeing how they were put to death with a butchers knife in a quick fashion and without contemplation, especially the poor pigs. Their screams could be heard a mile away!

The pigs would be slaughtered on Sundays very early in the

morning so the family could enjoy fresh meat at a special dinner the same day with my grandfather presiding at the large dining table surrounded by the big family. My grandfather, Florentino Munoz, who was born in a little town named "Piedras Gordas," usually dressed very formally in a navy blue suit with a vest and his dignified and imposing figure displayed authority. None of his grandchildren, especially me, would dare to disturb dinner. At the end of dinner all the children made a line to receive from our grandfather our allowance (three cents) which we used to go to the near by kiosk at the Alameda to buy candy.

The house had a big traditional Mexican kitchen with a wood oven where all the animal products were prepared and in a remote corner of the smoky kitchen, milk from my grandfather's ranch was processed into cheese, butter, and yogurt. I still have very vivid memories of the delicious smell of the fresh food being cooked, of the tortillas being made by hand at the very same moment, and of the different kinds of chile sauces, including foaming hot chocolate with a stick of cinnamon that I still enjoy so much. All the aromas together permeated every room of the whole house!

But those were the times! What a life style and quality of life in those far away years, and what a contrast with the way we live now in modern society! It is evident that our society has suffered a change, but not for good. Where are all those values and family traditions that we used to enjoy so much?

Even the pace how we live in these days has changed. Everything we do now is fast. We eat fast food, we travel in fast jets, we communicate instantly with our computers and cell phones, we have fast access to information through the internet. Yes we live faster, but in spite of all this, are we more happy in the way we live now?

It is natural and logical to think that we want to be happy. From another angle we could ask who would not want to be happy. But the sad fact is that in our modern society millions of people in one way or another are unable to reach this goal. Just look at those people with long and aggressive faces walking on the streets in some big cities or even closer to us in our work with our colleagues.

In my more than thirty years working in the Mexican embassies and the consulates in different countries I experienced first hand on multiple occasions many of people who no matter what, were complaining all the time. As part of my responsibilities I had to listen to their complaints but I was able to differentiate those with real grievances from others that just did it because they were in a state of constant frustration and unhappiness. You don't have to be a psychologist to be able to tell one from another. The same happened with some of my bosses but they expressed their unhappiness abusing their positions of authority. It is difficult when we have to deal on a daily basis with this kind of people.

But there is other harder evidences of unhappiness around us. The use of illegal drugs, especially among young people, and the epidemic of obesity. Both problems combined are becoming one of the biggest challenges for modern society. It is widely known that people turn to drugs as a rapid and easy way to achieve happiness in an artificial form with the wrong belief that happiness is something they can inject, drink, smoke or inhale through their noses. They do not care about the high price they have to pay for hurting themselves and their families. Society pays in terms of the proliferation of particularly perverse and violent criminals because of the profitable illegal drug market, which is also a natural consequence of the atmosphere of lack of morals and the collapse of legality.

But there are other complex repercussions derived from this problem. It is known that the growing power of the drug cartels is a direct threat to the governments in some countries for the challenge to their capacity to provide security to their own citizens. What is happening with the unstoppable wave of killings in Ciudad Juarez, Mexico, speaks by itself. Another scary situation which is being created is the connection of the drug producing countries in some parts of the world, Afghanistan among them, and the financing of the groups engaged in international terrorism. No one could deny that all this is making a more dangerous and turbid world.

In the case of obesity we have to make a just distinction and separate the clear cases when it is produced by hormonal and physiological imbalances. But in some others it is evident that it becomes associated with being trapped in a society that works against and contradicts the real concept of what is real happiness. These are people that are driven to use food to fulfill the moral and psychological needs that come from a sense of emptiness and dissatisfaction as a result of living under the influence of a distorting materialistic society of consumerism. They become convinced that their needs can be compensated with eating more and more. Quantity becomes more important than quality and balance.

In reinforcing the above, the structures of the current system of food supply don't leave many choices to those who would like to escape the trap of the fast and junk food industry. Just look at the panorama of fast food restaurants and the gigantic advertisements with bright colors that fill the horizon any place we go.

What makes things worse is the irony of progress with all the technological means of locomotion that save people from having to walk or to climb, and the artificial control of just the right temperature in homes, offices or cars, which brings other physical consequences to their bodies. These people don't burn calories any more by moving or having to adjust their body temperature so their calories are saved and stored in form of fats which adds to the consequent decrease of their metabolism. With the excessive consumption of energy to avoid any effort for mobility or transportation and using air conditioners and heaters all the time, they are hurting themselves in two ways. First, storing in their bodies all the calories saved from physical effort and living in total comfort, and second, degrading our environment with the excessive use of energy.

An indirect effect is the destructive mentality of not doing exercise any more because now it is so simple to move and live in total comfort with all these means of technology, with the convenient conclusion that we don't need a fit body anymore to get where we want to go or achieve what represents for us instantaneous pleasure and reward. Just look at the new generation of children seated in front of their TV sets playing electronic games pretending that they are participating in different sport competitions or war games but the only physical effort required is moving their fingers and mouths to play and simultaneously gulping soft drinks loaded with sugar and popcorn covered with plenty of butter. They don't have to move their bodies anymore to enjoy their childhood. How distant is this image of an exuberant and happy youngster as the one portrayed in The Adventures of Tom Sawyer!

This apparent panacea of progress ironically makes the individual more unhappy because of the distorted shape of their bodies that result. But even worse, because it affects their whole health condition beginning with diabetes, heart problems, blindness, cancer, amputations, and in severe cases, even their capacity to move by themselves, causing them to remain in bed or dependent on self propelled wheel chairs.

The other pandemic we are seeing more and more in our days are people with depression. This sad problem may very well be a necessary consequence of all the disruptions and moral confusion of society as the real cause of the unhappiness of the individual who naturally feels depressed. We would be surprised to find out the proportion of cases of depression which do not necessarily respond to a real condition of molecular imbalances in the brain that are being treated from a simplistic medical angle with prescriptions of expensive and addictive pills. There cannot be chemical solutions to moral problems!

These pandemic health problems have two costly repercussions in our society. First, in the huge expense and overburden of the medical systems in dealing with the treatment of the different illnesses derived from such grave conditions. Second are the negative effects in productivity because of the days lost in work when these people call in sick on a regular basis. The last payer of these endemic problems is the economy as a whole. Ironically, the same society that sets up this situation.

I could continue with an endless list of other sad and troubling examples of unhappiness and dissatisfaction in individuals, like alcoholism, the increasing rate of suicides, and the bloody and senseless killings in schools or in public places by dangerous people who can buy any amount and all kinds of lethal weapons with no restrictions.

It's shocking to watch the daily news saturated with every detail of the bloodshed produced by these kinds of massacres. Unfortunately the publicity built around this news seems to promote the violent outbursts of these empty and angry people who are willing to trade without a trace of remorse their lives and the lives of as many innocents they can kill for the instantaneous notoriety they gain.

These kind of situations are not limited to a particular country. They are found all around the world, thanks to globalization. In these days there is not a single nation that is free from this kind of social decomposition. We cannot be proud of negative equalization!

Of course the obvious goal of progress has been to create the material basis for better living conditions of the individual which is perfectly reasonable and legitimate. However, using intelligence without moral references and wisdom as a way to shape society places several obstacles on the road to happiness in this life.

Man should not be his own victim. Society has to conform to our authentic needs defined by our transcendental purpose in a way that at the end it can become an effective support for the pursuit of happiness of the individual and not an obstacle!

"Happiness is the meaning and the purpose of life, the whole aim and end of human existence."

- Aristotle

CHAPTER 12

WHAT IS REAL HAPPINESS?

In recollecting my school years I especially remember my professor of History of Philosophy at the "Instituto de Ciencias de Zacatecas", Uriel Marquez, who no doubt has been the best teacher I ever had because he taught me how to rely on philosophy and history to understand the main concepts in the fundamental questions related to humankind. He had the special virtue of arousing in his students an interest in learning through his vivid description of the main philosophers in world history. As if he were using a colorful video about them, he showed us the human behind the thinker and the historical circumstances during which they lived. He also taught us how to think to the point of burning our brains!

I was only14 years old but I felt very proud of being a student of the most prestigious school of the city of Zacatecas where I lived at that age with its excellent body of teachers, very much in tune with the integral education of the students, including a very strong athletic program. They made us sweat in every angle of our education but we were very motivated with our intellectual and physical growth.

To be well prepared for my class at ten in the morning with professor Marquez every day I climbed to the top of the mountain"La Bufa", not too high, maybe fifteen hundred feet of altitude. I had the time to do that because my previous class, algebra, ended at eight o' clock so I would have an hour to go and come back and have an extra hour to study. I enjoyed being up there alone with the cold wind blowing in my face with the view of the city below and with plenty of blood rushing into my brain to fully concentrate in my intellectual pursuit. Sometimes my cousin and best friend, Beto Villa accompanied me.

Once the class would start I was ready, practically fired up with so many questions for my teacher, trying to understand how the different philosophers tackled our most important concerns that make up our human dimension such as the concept of happiness. It was not until a few years later with my close encounter with death that I found the essential element to be able to respond to this important question to myself. Happiness is so important for humans that throughout all our history we have been engaged in building a complex social structure to achieve that elusive goal, but as we have seen before in the previous chapter, it has not always resulted as planned. Ironically it would seem that contemporary society is reversing the attempt to achieve happiness.

How many people do we know, who having spent all of their lives in their ambition to have power, money, material possessions, nobility titles, or political positions when reaching the end of their lives find that the only thing left for them is anguish and fears? Especially when in their frenzy to achieve all that they had to trade in their integrity and moral values when choosing pats.

This frenetic appetite of people in pursuit of wealth, power, and material possessions is a fruitless pretense of happiness. It is like the greedy King Midas who, after being able to convert everything he touched into gold, died of starvation totally frustrated because he could not eat the food that he had converted into the shiny metal!

On one side social structures do not correspond to the dimension of human psyche. In the last instance the individual participating in the design of social structure doesn't know what real happiness means. It is like trying to make a suit for someone in a dark room where we are unable to take precise body measurements.

The concept of happiness has been profoundly analyzed by the Greek philosophers, mainly by Aristotle, in my view, the greatest universal thinker of all time. From an integrated perspective he recognized that happiness is based on our material circumstances, as well as on our virtues. This concept of happiness recognizes that moral values are important to achieve but also implies that we are composed of matter and spirit, opening the road to the perception of God. As it is known Aristotle thought that happiness is the ultimate goal of humans, and he believed in a happy medium in all things to achieve this ultimate state.

Another Greek philosopher, Epicurus, also tackled the concept. This humble philosopher, well known for being congruent in his way of life with his own principles, believed that happiness in its highest form was achieved only with the pursuit of modest pleasures derived from natural needs to be free from frustration. In other words, practicing frugality. However as it is known Epicureanism is often misinterpreted as a form of Hedonism in the mentality of contemporary times by our materialistic society of sensual excesses and the pursuit of pure pleasure. What Epicurus believed was that the main portion of our material wishes are banalities so when we cannot reach them, frustration results. What this proponent had in mind was the satisfaction of only natural needs and a simple way of life. I would say, "Simplicity is good and beautiful."

Incidentally, following this line of thought I have a rule to follow when I go to the stores and have the strong temptation to buy a particular item, I say to myself, " Is it indispensable?" Only if I can respond to this question saying yes with all honesty then I buy it. This is a tremendous shield we can use to fight consumerism, saving money but above all, saving limited resources, especially these days when we have to have in mind the concept of sustainability because of the needs of those coming after us. It is also a good way to practice self-restraint and temperance.

St. Augustine, one of the key figures in the transition from classical antiquity to the Middle Ages, said that it is the essential subject of philosophy to teach men how to attain happiness, and deal with the subject in contrast with the concept of evil. "No one is happy unless he has all he wants and wants nothing that is evil." In this concept, St. Augustine's mind reflects the essence of his monumental work, "The City of God," where the human quest is defined by the struggle between good and evil.

More contemporary philosophers like the tower of German Idealism, Immanuel Kant, also directed a portion of his investigations toward the analysis of the concept of happiness. However this outstanding philosopher, author of "The Critique of Pure Reason", who despite being construed to his trust in pure reason, after all, accepted the belief in God based in moral proof and dealt with the elusive subject of happiness, but only in a tangential way. He concluded that happiness is a state of affairs proportioned to virtue.

In our days, philosophy has practically abandoned the subject, leaving the door opened to science and materialism to fill the vacuum in determining what is relevant in this fundamental pursuit of humankind.

Researchers in brain science, using the advances of Magnetic Resonance Images combined with computers, are peeping inside the brain to see if they find what is happiness. What they can see with this technology are only images of the areas of the brain which become activated like the lights of a christmas tree when the individual feels happy. This is taking them to the wrong interpretation that they are discovering happiness as if it were a little mouse turning on the neurons in our brains. Obviously they confuse pleasure with happiness.

The fact is that these scientific tools are effectively showing researchers aspects of the functioning of the brain identifying those neuronal areas where our emotions take place and link with the muscles of our face and body to express those sentiments. But we have to be clear and ask if this approach, that no doubt is opening new ways for understanding and treating many mental disorders with the mapping of the brain, will find what happiness is.

With the advancement of science we could expect the additional use of quantum mechanics. However, considering how the realm of the quantum phenomena interacts with our human scale it may be possible to find out that our brain activity is not necessarily confined only to the areas inside the skull. When that happens, then it will be interesting to find where happiness is located according to this scientific research trying to deal with a subjectively moral concept which cannot be explained by MRIS.

This would add to the discussion over whether or not the advance of science is linear. With the baffling discoveries of science in the last years some seem to confirm more and more to me that our collective belief about the realm of the transcendental is joining with what science is finding. The circle closes!

But at this point it should be noted that in spite of all that has been done to identify what is happiness, so far nobody can tell us precisely what it is. All they have done is tell us the how but not the what it is, as is the case with Aristotle who indicated the road to happiness, and Kant, who aimed to the heart of the matter. But his definition, as I said before, only touches the concept in a tangential way. The rest of the discussion has been limited to the different ways and the conditions to reach an indeterminate concept of happiness in this world without concluding about its ultimate concept and definition.

The problem is, as it also happens with other fundamental questions linked to humankind, we need to determine an appropriate frame of reference which in this case is the acceptance of the concept of God with the totality of its implications in our life. This way we will be able to understand who we are and how we are integrated as humans so we can see what it means for us in a holistic perspective the concept of happiness.

The question of who we are is resolved with our reference to God as our creator. We are basically composed of His same substance which is love, but at the same time because our present reality is given in a material world, our substance is not pure. It is mixed with matter and subjected to the elements of nature including the laws of nature, and for that reason we are not perfect as God.

As human beings we are integrated in a mixed formula. We have a material body (with our physical senses), a brain (intelligence) and mind (our soul) all working interconnected to give us the capacity to make sense of this world and ourselves. Our body, with its physical senses (sight, sound, smell, touch, taste), gather the information that surround us which is processed by our intelligence in the brain and gives us an interpretation of our material reality. Our mind connects our spiritual essence with our Creator so we can reach human consciousness of who we are and what is our purpose.

Having an image of humanity in the previous context, we can now try to define what happiness is. Our mind that serves the purpose of connecting our godly substance with our material expression when we are dying disconnects totally from our body to be able to evolve through the different stages of the process of death. Through this process, not only do we maintain the previous level of human consciousness, but it expands to the level of total consciousness (as it happened to me) to reach the final point of merging with God. This, to me, is real and absolute happiness, the state we reach at the pinnacle of our process of death absorbed into the pure and loving essence of our Creator for eternity!

In the meantime, here on earth, while we wait for that wonderful moment to happen we can try to reach a previous level of happiness in anticipation of the moment of truth that we will face. But the basis is the same, we need our basic reference with our Creator as the cause and purpose of our life and our own reality. With the connection of our mind with our bodies and brain intelligence the level of consciousness we can reach in this world about God and our final destiny with Him, should guide and conform our lives towards Him as our purpose.

That level of consciousness, human consciousness, will also produce in us a state of happiness that will be perfected and completed when we finally join God in his realm. But if we want to have a tangible proof of this on earth all we have to do is see those individuals around us who already have found and accepted God. They are those people, who regardless of their economic or social status, display a higher quality of life marked by love and compassion as a direct reflection of having reached their state of real happiness!

"The keenest sorrow is to recognize ourselves as the sole cause of all our adversities."

- Sophocles

"I do not believe that God has imposed suffering upon anyone to punish them or teach them a lesson."

- Ernest Holmes

CHAPTER 13

IF GOD LOVES US, WHY DOES HE ALLOW SUFFERING IN THIS WORLD?

Through my diplomatic work I interacted indirectly with two of the individuals who will be remembered in modern history because of the extent of suffering they caused their own people in their countries.

One was Idi Amin, who as President of Uganda at the time I was a member of the Mexican delegation to the General Assembly of The United Nations (UN) in 1975. He visited in his position of Head of State the universal organization in New York. In those days he already was well known to everybody because the many assassinations and atrocities he had committed against his own people (the estimate is around five hundred thousand).

I was outside of the General Assembly auditorium writing a report to my delegation about the relevant parts of the speeches of the Heads of State, when I felt someone approaching me to my right. There he was, the towering and impressive figure of Idi Amin followed by two body guards. He was near seven feet tall and two hundred and fifty pounds of pure muscle, pitch black as the darkest night, with a round face and with his piercing eyes looking at me. I wondered why. Honestly, in all my life I have never been more fearful of a person. That was Idi Amin. His eyes reflected evil!

The other individual was Nicaraguan dictator Anastasio Somosa, whom I didn't meet personally. In 1979 I was Alternate Representative of Mexico at The Organization of the American States (OAS). Somosa had ordered the killings against the people involved in a revolution to oust him. The OAS declared his massive atrocities to be considered genocide against the people of Nicaragua and such declaration supported by another resolution of the United Nations determined his ousting from his country. The active role of the Mexican delegation at the OAS headed by the outstanding Mexican Foreign Minister Jorge Castaneda y Alvarez de la Rosa, was the pivotal factor in reaching such declaration.

Incidentally, on these two occasions I had the privilege of working with two of the greatest diplomats in the modern history of the Mexican Foreign Service. The head of the Mexican Mission to the United Nations at the time was Alfonso Garcia

Robles, who was awarded the Nobel Peace Prize for his determinant role in the promotion and negotiation of the Treaty of Tlatelolco which prohibits nuclear weapons in the Latin American and Caribean region. And my boss at the OAS, Rafael de la Colina, who has been the oldest and wisest diplomat of the Mexican Foreign Service. He became the effective pillar of the OAS for more than twenty years until his retirement at the age of 87. He was called with reverence "El Maestro." With Ambassador de la Colina who, besides being a great diplomat was above all a special human being, I had the special opportunity of building a personal relationship. He was our Godfather in our wedding and also the Godfather in the baptism of my son Ricardo. He used to comment to friends that he considered me his adopted son.

For their important work for the good of humanity these two diplomats provide a stark contrast to those two dictators mentioned above who inflicted so much suffering to so many people.

On too many occasions we hear of situations that take place around us or in other countries involving a great suffering of many innocent people in wars, revolutions, terrorism, economic meltdowns, climate change, poverty, drugs, abductions, and killings, etc. It is overwhelming to watch the news everyday emphasizing these kinds of tragedies. Sometimes it would seem preferable just to unplug the TV and get lost in the most remote place in Alaska. But this is our reality every single day. The fact is that even if we wanted we could not close our eyes to what is going in the world.

There is so much exposure to suffering that our society is becoming insensitive to it. Suffering even seems to be a symbol of our times. Some people say that since the early times of history suffering has been a part of life and that if we see how the conditions of the world are getting more complicated today due to increased population and climate change on a global scale, such problems should signal a worsening of the situation for our future. With a view like that, past, present, and future together should indicate that this bleak panorama is a constant condition of our life in this world.

How many individuals have influenced history but not necessarily for their contributions to humanity or for their good actions? As some examples, Adolph Hitler could be at the top of the list for having ordered the murder of more than six million Jews, Joseph Stalin who massacred about nine million of his own people, Idi Amin in Uganda who also killed a large number in his country (including his pregnant wife), the Nicaraguan dictator Anastasio Somosa, who also committed genocide against his own people. We could continue with this list of criminals that earned the dubious privilege of forming part of the modern history of mankind for the extreme suffering they produced.

The level of horror and suffering that these monsters of humanity inflicted on so many innocent people frequently is mentioned in the arguments that some individuals use to blame God for allowing suffering. They believe that God should be using His love and power to stop this from happening. Still others even say that the suffering in the world is proof that God does not exist.

It is very clear that what these individuals really want to do with their unjust criticism is to erode the image of God or dismiss the idea of his reality. The answer that can be given to these skeptics is that the magnitude and purity of God's love towards us is such that in our creation, He wanted to bring us not only into reality, but loving us so much, He made us in His own image with all the virtues that confirm His substance of love, intelligence, and harmony. And among those virtues, He included the freedom of choice, our will to act.

We humans can make our own decisions, to choose with our actions whether we use the framework of values and principles derived from the image of our Father like the virtue of love and its complement, compassion. This necessarily implies that we will not cause any kind of suffering to others and that we should have solidarity and responsibility towards those in need.

However, if we choose not to love others it will be very easy for us to fall under the influence of our lowest evil inclinations and kill, torture, rape, lie, cheat, hoard, steal from others, pollute and cause all kind of suffering to our brothers and sisters for whatever reason. Power without moral direction can be lethal.

In balance the lessons of history don' t let us hide the shameful fact that humankind has employed more of its time and more resources through all the centuries in killing and causing suffering to each other in bloody wars than in any other endeavor, but it seems that we have not learned any lessons from the bloodshed. In modern times we are still being followed by the grim shadow of our self destruction with the threats of wars and terrorism. Just take a look at the new war machinery being built. It is undeniable that the biggest threat to our survival is us, ourselves!

But in all this God does not intervene because His love is granting us that freedom to choose and act. Let's remember that what our Father wants for us all is our absolute happiness beginning in this world. A happiness that is going to be accomplished only when we decide that is what we want. He doesn't impose His love on us. That would not be love.

It does not mean that God closes His eyes to our suffering. He has already provided us with the tools and the means to avoid any suffering. But He has left it in our hands to choose so it is our responsibility to make goodness prevail and virtue over evil and bad instincts using the higher values that we possess as children of God to make our world a better place.This is the quest for humankind.

When suffering is inflicted to others it is because we let the beast inside us loose allowing evil to prevail over goodness!

"Justice is the constant and perpetual will to allot to every man his due."

- Domitus Ulpian

CHAPTER 14

JUDGMENT DAY

During the process of my death when I made the distinction between what I thought was an object that I encountered in that absolute vacuum and what in fact resulted instead in a being, was an amazing turning point. I was no longer alone in that state of nothingness. The unidentified being and I were two concrete realities in the middle of the absolute emptiness. The nothing was transformed into a different situation by the presence of somebody else. It was a change of phase into something new.

In the successive moment that followed, the growth of that being coming from very far away towards me at a fantastic speed, allowed me to be aware of His immense power expressed in a form of light and living energy. At that moment when I was at the stage of being absorbed completely in his substance my expanded consciousness made me know without any doubt who that extraordinary being of love was. Obviously I exploded with joy and happiness when I realized that my destiny was to become one with Him for eternity. The last stage of my final destiny was taking place and I was incredibly aware of what was happening!

An important moment in the process that I was so fortunate to experience was the precise moment when our loved Creator convinced me that He was giving me His unconditional love without demanding anything from me in reciprocity.This made me feel that I could have arrived at that transcendental moment with some imperfections and faults on my shoulders (sins), nevertheless He accepted me and loved me. Our experience here on earth in our role of parents should help us to understand this heavenly situation.

God created us in the reality of this universe with souls, material bodies and limited intelligence. It is a mixture that makes us imperfect entities while we live in this world. However, He is there in His purest essence of love waiting for us as our destiny to be transformed into perfect entities as He is. All this represents nothing less than the highest achievement of an absolute state of happiness that our minds can conceive!

The fact of my return to this world was only because I became overwhelmed by this amazing truth and asked for a second opportunity so I could thank God by doing something of value for Him as a tangible demonstration of my reciprocal love for Him. It was not for another reason such as I had felt there was a conditioning on His part demanding to correct my imperfections or a sense of guilt from me. What I honestly felt was only an intense love born in me at that moment and that I still wanted to have another opportunity to express my love and gratitude in a concrete form.

But it must be asked, does my experience somehow mean that we are not going to be judged by God with our baggage of good and bad actions in life? Will it mean that all those who have killed, tortured, stolen, lied, raped, etc, will find their way into heaven because God is not going to judge and punish them?

Having been so close to our Creator, I was able to feel that his essence of love is so big and so pure that there wouldn't be room at all for any judgment to take place. It is the kind of love that would forgive anything. I became convinced that we were created by this beautiful being with the sole purpose of our absolute happiness.

On the other hand, my conviction is that humankind was not brought into existence to be punished or destroyed if we don't pass the test. God created us with the purpose to give us absolute happiness that implies forgiving our imperfections.

It is precisely for not demanding our Creator from us that we have to be perfect to be allowed into Heaven that He does not establish limitations to give us His love. But the same notion of not imposing limitations on us implies something extremely valuable, freedom, the capacity to decide. Even to the point to be able to chose whether or not we want the amazing destiny of merging with Him for eternity. He does not impose his love. He offers it. So we have a choice.

His love is so big and so pure that he doesn't ask us to accept it. He becomes our destiny when we freely embrace it. But there

THE LIGHT AT THE END OF DARKNESS

is the possibility that some people, having reached a state of degradation because of their reproachable actions, or others, because of their egos and arrogance, see themselves as self-centered, different from God, and decide that they do not want to become absorbed as part of His substance. Evil doesn't relate to goodness.

In this case their decision would be granted. Those individuals would be simply sent instantly to another destination without God. <u>This way they would be bringing justice to themselves.</u> As has been described by St. Augustine, and I agree totally with this concept, Hell is the absence of God. This way justice would be achieved by their own judgment, by their own hands. It would be the Perfect Justice!

"We look forward to the time when the Power of Love will replace the Love of Power. Then will our world know the blessings of peace."

- William Gladstone

CHAPTER 15

OUR APPETITE FOR POWER

When I was going through the process of death I encountered myself completely alone, suspended in an absolute vacuum that can only be described as the nothingness. I remained there expectant for a moment without knowing what was to happen next. I did not know if that was going to be the end of my journey through death or not. It was an absolute feeling of remaining alone with absolutely nothing or anyone else around me. But the strange situation made me more aware than ever of my own reality. I was dead, that's how I felt!

When we live on this earth we are surrounded by forces, light, sounds, objects, people, and of course we feel movement so we have the sensation of time. But in that suspended stage there was no movement or time. The nothingness! These elements are here in our material reality as part of our daily life but they are gone completely in that stage of our process of death.

Despite my bewilderment for being suspended in that situation and not knowing the outcome, I didn't experience any real fear. I realized that I was facing death but I had faith that something would change in that situation. We cling to our faith in such moments to overcome the tremendous fear that otherwise could overwhelm us!

I mention this because what happened next was an amazing contrast. I faced the most tremendous power imaginable when God appeared, first from very far away as a little particle of energy. When He approached me at a very high speed I was able to feel His real energy and tremendous power. It seems clear to me that one of the reasons why we get to meet Him removed from our material bodies is that otherwise we would be totally obliterated in a thousand pieces when facing at that point His overwhelming presence.

At that moment without any doubt I knew who created the universe. I was perfectly aware that the power of the universe and its energy come from our Father. This power beyond description was beginning to absorb me so I could identify the nature of His essence. The tremendous dimension of power I was facing was made by a harmonic combination of infinite intelligence and living energy, all together expressed in the power of His love. Fortunately, at that impressive moment we have all the capacity needed to identify such amazing reality in its full manifestation: our new state of expanded consciousness.

When we experience the powers of nature here on earth such

as a hurricane, a tornado, an earthquake, a tsunami, a volcanic eruption, etc., we can have a taste of what the power of nature means. I also have had the opportunity to experience that kind of power with a hurricane in Acapulco and several big earthquakes in Mexico City.

When cosmologists describe the black holes in the center of the galaxies in the universe they speak in terms of the invincible attracting power these celestial bodies use to suck everything around them, including light. The black holes are the most powerful objects in the universe but not even cosmologists who are measuring and theorizing about these objects have a credible clue of what is the real extent of their power. And to think that the architect of all these wonders including the universe itself is God! That could give anyone an idea of the power I faced. That is real power but it is a positive and creative power. It is the power of love that created us!

Humans have an undeniable appetite for power. Many chapters of history have been written about the ancestral struggle for power but the lessons of history also tell us that power without a moral framework can be dangerous and destructive. And not only with those unlucky ones that have had the bad fortune to gotten in the way of the powerful, it mainly destroys the souls of the those who abuse it.

That is because humans have not learned how to make good use of power linked to our transcendental purpose. The usual purpose of the ambition to have power is to gain dominance and control of other people. Unfortunately history is full of these examples. Only in a very few instances power has been used by humankind for authentic leadership and for constructive and moral reasons.

But the ambition for power can reach even higher levels when it is used to build the egos of those wicked people that use it to compensate their low image and shortcomings they have of themselves. This is when power becomes irresistible and is used to feed the big egos becoming more addictive than drugs. How many names we can remember of those infamous big egos in history (invariably the name of Adolph Hitler comes to me) who became partners with evil to cause so much suffering to humankind with the power they gained.

We humans are not perfect entities and that imperfection makes us extremely susceptible to falling victim to a blinding use of power the wrong way to destroy, to lie, to hurt, to cause suffering, to abuse, to endanger, to be above others and above the law (moral and legal). It is the trap of a compensating feeling of superiority that blinds people who do not understand that we have been created equals so they pretend to control and to be above others.

Under the concept of ruling kings who falsely claimed to have been invested with powers from God to support their authority, such fabrication reinforced the mentality of superiority based in the dishonest and immoral justification of their powers. In some measure such mentality permeated to those people who were favored by those rulers giving place to build societies under the basis of a psyche of power and superiority over others.

When the Spanish conquerors representing the monarchy in Spain came to Mexico, they brought with them such a mentality as their main instrument of dominance and power, imposing a social structure sustained on the superiority of the conquerors. At a certain point they even tried to classify the defeated indians in the same category of animals.

Many centuries of struggle in Mexico have tried to get rid of such burden and the advances are undeniable. But the fact is that still many people, especially those less favored, have had to emigrate to other countries. The sad truth behind that phenomena is that many of those millions of poor Mexicans who leave the country not only do so for economic necessity. Deep down their hearts they want to give their children the opportunities they were denied in a society where the powerful still rule.

On a personal level, one of the situations that has put me to the test in this life was when I was tempted by the deceptive aromas of power just after graduating as a lawyer. I was offered very attractive "positions of power" in the business world in Mexico and I even had the opportunity to have a taste of it when I was offered a position as a partner of some very wealthy men in Mexico. Fortunately, by then I had already made my fundamental decision of what I wanted to do with my life so I declined.

Yes, I am afraid of the lure of power in this life because of what I learned about myself in my humbling experience with death but also because I have seen very close in too many instances what it does to real people. I could see it happen to many friends trapped by the high society of Mexico where an individual who wants to belong to the powerful elite has to live by its archaic rules of the game. The Mexican revolution did many wonderful things in building the basis of a modern Mexico but the rules and the mentality that shaped the high society in the era of Porfirio Diaz, the Mexican dictator who was ousted from the country one hundred years ago, have not changed much.

I witnessed something similar in my diplomatic life in the Foreign Service especially at the Mexican Embassy in Washington where I worked in the 1980s for five years as Political Counselor. Many of the members of the large staff of the Embassy were against each other all the time, involved in political machinations and bending over backward to gain favor with the powerful people visiting from Mexico including Mexican Presidents, members of the cabinet, and several other influential Mexican politicians who frequently came to visit. The Embassy in Washington is the traditional political trampoline to rapidly jump to positions of power in the Mexican Foreign Service. In that highly charged environment I could see how some people can easily be transformed into machiavellian individuals who can lose track in their lives thinking that power is everything for them in the world.

But all that is nothing compared with the present and apocalyptic dangers our fragile planet is facing in part because of other kind of individuals with immoral ambitions for economic power at a world level. Those who, with their insatiable economic interests, promote an unrestricted consumption of coal and oil over clean sources of energy with the devastating effects on the environment.

The other scary but real danger points mostly to the preservation of the basic nature of humans because of the blinding ambition for power of several unethical scientists who, with access to the fantastic advancement of high technology, pretend to tinker with the brain and genetics with total disregard for the consequences to the delicate and unique structure of the nature of humans designed by our Creator. It seems as if they would want to replace God in the designing of humankind.

One of the lessons that impacted me most as a child was in my religion class my mother made me take. It was the story of how Lucifer became an evil being after he had enjoyed great power as the favorite angel of God. Luzbel sat to the right of God until he decided that he was so special, beautiful and powerful that he could take the place of God. The outcome of his arrogance and defiance is well known by everybody well versed in the Old Testament, he was sent to sit in the ugly caverns of Hell forever transformed as Lucifer.

The infinite power of God comes from the convergence of His infinite energy, intelligence, and harmony which all together makes His essence of love. If an individual in this life cannot comprehend and accept the nature of the authentic power of God which is love then his appetite for power will sink him along with those who chose the other way!

"Never, never, never give up."

- Winston Churchill

CHAPTER 16

THE MEANING OF EFFORT WITH GOD IN OUR LIVES

One early morning when getting up from bed to go to work (before I used that time to pray in the mornings), I felt my daily routine as something heavy and unpleasant. It was a cold morning and I had to do my exercises, have breakfast, get dressed, and leave in a hurry, but above all, tons of work and a difficult boss were waiting for me at the office.

At that time we lived in Ecuador and despite the embassy there being small, my boss wanted to make it look very important and he held all kinds of social events to attract important figures of the government and the high society of Quito. I was the deputy so I was responsible for their organization to the last detail and had to remain at those receptions all night until they ended, sometimes at five in the morning. But the worst is that I don't drink, don't smoke, and don't dance. Not all diplomatic work has to do with substantial affairs. I even had started looking for another job, I was close to giving up.

That made me question why our lives are such an effort. I remained seated for a few moments in bed thinking about it, trying to identify some time in my life that making an effort would had not have been an unpleasant thing for me, but I could not. Always that unpleasant feeling accompanied my efforts, including in distant times when I was a little boy and had to get up early and my mother literally had to drag me from bed to go to school. My own answer was that the idea had to have some significance. I started digging into my question so it would make sense to me. But at that moment I was in a hurry, my boss was waiting for me at the office and I do not like to be late, so I decided to leave the thought for another occasion.

After a while, but not forgetting my determination to reach a conclusion about the idea that I had about this unpleasant feeling associated with effort, I looked at the different moments and circumstances when I was presented with this feeling. This way I was able to confirm that effort was present with me all the time, not only related to school or work or exercise, but associated with every other aspect of my life in particular with moral effort, when we are tempted to do things that do not fit in the framework of our moral life. However, at that point I observed that a constant element had to be associated with the idea of effort. That was purpose. I started to find the strings of the problem!

In the animal kingdom effort is more obvious. It comes with the imperative to get food to survive. Of course, this is something we share completely with all the other living species around us.

However that is as far as we can get in comparing humans with the other species in that respect. In our particular case the array of opportunities for making an effort come with the complexity of our human essence and the volume of activities we do to pursue our important purpose to reach God.

We are the manifestation of a material and spiritual unity that makes us humans. We are beings made of a biological body and a brain, in conjunction with a mind. We must feed ourselves, not only with food and material products for our bodies, but with the kind of food that suits our human qualities, with a special food made of material and moral ingredients combined in harmony to support our efforts in trying to reach perfection in the image we have of our Creator.

It was with this perspective that I began to understand how, if we bring God in our lives, everything we do in this world with effort regardless of how heavy and hard can be we can transform it in our passion.

If we can understand this and accept participation in the project of God for humanity using our effort then that concept will be transformed instead into the concept of vitality and unlimited energy which is in the substance of God, shared with us through our soul.

This way our effort will no longer represent an unpleasant and difficult feeling for us. On the contrary, it will become the key to channel the infinite energy that comes from God to never give up in our purpose in life!

123

"The fear of death follows from the fear of life. A man who lives fully is prepared to die at any time."
- Mark Twain

CHAPTER 17

NO ROOM FOR FEARS

When my throat closed because of the anaphylactic allergic reaction to the clump of cat hair I swallowed with my soup, I was initially able to remain calm because of the way of life I had followed up until then. I got thrills with danger and was not scared of anything including swimming in the open ocean with sharks, climbing steep rocks with my bare hands, exploring abandoned mines and especially driving like crazy at full speed. I was very young, between fourteen and fifteen (no driver license yet), but I was already dreaming and making plans to become a race driver. I knew that nobody would beat me because I was not afraid of sticking the pedal to the bottom and keeping it there until I would win, as I did at the street competitions (of course my parents didn't know about this).

At that young age I felt indestructible and my idea of death was somehow attractive as an opportunity to show off. I enjoyed adventure and I remember how much I liked the taste of adrenalin in my mouth!

But when two minutes passed without being able to breath at all, I was still struggling to keep my calm, knowing that I could hold until two minutes without air and my throat should open soon. Though that did not happen!

Then the crude reality struck me like a hammer in my head. The tangibility of death combined with the tremendous desperation for the need of air was a reality I never experienced before. I got up from the chair in a violent move with my mouth wide open trying to run in desperation to nowhere. I can imagine now the look of real fear in my face and the big scare for my grandmother, my brother and my aunts who were watching me in total shock.

At that moment I knew what real fear meant for the first time in my life. It is the most horrible feeling anybody can imagine, produced in great part by the idea of becoming extinct forever in conjunction with the stress and pain transmitted to every cell of our body.

Let' s remember that pain is a safeguard we have in our bodies handled by our brains which is reflected in the form of fear by our powerful instinct of survival. It works like a mechanism of emergency that is activated when our brain identifies a critical situation that could produce the cessation of life. This strong instinct in itself is convenient to have because when we do not have it in our brushes with death, we could destroy our bodies completely and the possibility of a return would be impossible.

Sometimes the idea comes to me that if I had not gone

through that experience the way I was living my life, not knowing what fear meant, I could have ended not only dying anyway at my early age but I could have destroyed my body completely. For example if a shark decided to have me for dinner, my return to this world would be impossible because I would not have a body any more.

The opportunity I had to come back to live a new life with a purpose was thanks to God granting it to me. Obviously I needed a functional body that would not make it impossible to reconnect with my soul. In my case it is evident that the lack of air I experienced for about five minutes was not to the level of having produced an irreversible damage to my brain. For this reason I feel even more grateful with my Father.

But the kind of fear I experienced in those initial moments of the process of my death went away and I regained my calm after I disconnected from my body and did not feel the need to continue with the dependence of my body and breathing to maintain my full consciousness. I felt relieved to have left my body, but amazingly I also was aware that my consciousness had expanded which reassured me that death after all does not mean extinction of our being.

After that I came to another stage where I remained suspended in an absolute nothingness, retaining my calm but with a certain bewilderment at the same time for not knowing what would happen next. Thinking about that moment now makes me feel that somehow I should have felt at least some fear because of the mind blowing situation I was experiencing being in "the nothing". But I did not feel any fear because of my faith!

I am also aware that it sounds paradoxical to say that something like the "nothingness" was very real at the same time, but it was because I was there as a real and the only existent entity to sense it. Not light, not energy, not sound, not gravity, not even time--nothing. I was completely alone, suspended in that absolute void so I should have been afraid of the possibility of remaining forever in that situation.

A possible rational explanation for not feeling much fear at that moment could very well be that being disconnected from my body, the biological mechanism of fear with our instinct of survival could not function for the same reason of the disconnection. Besides, I was completely convinced with my expanded consciousness that I had not become extinct as I was afraid would occur when I still was going through the physical sensation of dying. However, I believe that the real reason for not being afraid in that circumstance was because somehow I had faith that the odd situation should change.

Obviously the next phase of the process produced less fear in me. I left behind that unique situation of nothingness to go to the other extreme: my encounter with our Creator. Only if we were to remain with some traces of our previous material reality, then with every reason we should be afraid not because of His essence which is pure love, but because He is projected to us with his tremendous reality of power and energy, so enormously overwhelming, that if we were to remain with our biological bodies as we are in this life we would be disintegrated instantaneously in a thousand pieces.

On the other hand, the fear of God we have here on earth due to our faults and imperfections does not have any reason to remain with us once we are there in His realm because of His unconditional and absolute love. I felt very reassuringly that His immense love embraces us completely when we accept Him so at the end in our destiny there is no room for any fears.

God created us, His children, with His love to make us happy in the most magnificent way imaginable in Heaven together with Him. That is our destiny. We all eventually will die and go through the inescapable process of death to join our Father who will be waiting for us with open arms despite our imperfections, not demanding anything from us, and much less, with any possibility of inflicting harm or punishment.

However the only reason left for the possibility of fear in this condition would be if blinded by our arrogance and self-centeredness, we believe that we do not need God because we are self sufficient and powerful enough. If we decide that there is no God or construct our lives with no God, then in that unique situation there would be a real and definite reason to be afraid. If in the final moment of truth facing God, He sees this as our desire to not accept Him we would be sent without delay to another destination where God will not be.

In a situation like that who can tell what the individual who rejects God is going to face. It could be total extinction or something even more horrible to conceive but the only sure thing will be that having rejected God that individual would have lost every possibility to be together with Him for evermore!

THE LIGHT AT THE END OF DARKNESS

PART THREE

THE THREE PILLARS OF KNOWLEDGE UNIFIED BY ONE TRUTH

"The ultimate reason of things must lie in a necessary substance, in which the differentiation of the changes only exists eminently as in their source; and this is what we call God.. God alone is the primary unity, or original simple substance, from which all monads, created and derived are produced."

- Gottfried Leibniz

"I love you when you bow in your mosque, kneel in your temple, pray in your church. For you and I are sons of one religion, and it is the spirit."

- Kahlil Gibran

CHAPTER 18

THE ROLE OF RELIGION IN SHOWING US THE ROAD

My mother was a very religious person as most mothers are in Mexico. When we moved from Zacatecas to live in Mexico City, my mother told us that all the family should go to pay a visit to La Villa de Guadalupe, which is the shrine where the image of The Virgin of Guadalupe is kept in a golden frame for people to pray to.

According to tradition, on December 12th, 1531, only a few years after the Spanish conquest of Mexico was accomplished by Hernan Cortez, the virgin appeared to the humble Indian Juan Diego, imprinting her image on his clothes, on the zarape he was wearing.

The particular feature of this virgin is her dark skin as the skin color of the Indians. She is an Indian virgin despite that she also depicts European features. Because of this particular mixture, especially the Indians and the mestizos identify with her. The rituals they perform at La Villa de Guadalupe for her are a mixture of religious Indian and Catholic rituals. Humbly they call her "Mi Virgencita." She became the linking factor between two religious worlds and a powerful symbol of the integration of two cultures.

Indians and mestizos in big numbers come from all over the country visit La Villa to pay their respects to their virgin. It is appealing to see them come walking alongside the roads in "Peregrinaciones," large caravans of a religious character that can take several days. Especially in the month of December, they come to Mexico City in those caravans to celebrate the apparition of the virgin. Very easily the city increases its population with one million people of those visitors.

The symbol of the Virgin Of Guadalupe is so important that when the movement for the independence of Mexico was started by Padre Miguel Hidalgo on September 16, 1810, he carried a flag with the image of the Virgin of Guadalupe. Of course, it is not difficult to understand why the majority of women in the country are named Guadalupe, as they are closely identified with the Virgin of Guadalupe. However there are also many Marias, those who identify more with the European Virgin Mary. My mother's name was Rosa Maria.

In those difficult moments when I realized that I was facing an inevitable death and a tremendous fear was descending over me, the image of the Cross somehow came to my mind as an expression that my faith would not let me alone in those critical moments.

Such a feeling certainly gave me the indispensable moral support that I greatly needed when everything pointed to my sure death, vanishing forever. At the same time it gave me the opportunity to build my hope that whatever was about to come would not be the end for me. My faith contained in such visualization at those moments certainly helped me counterbalance the feeling of intense terror produced by the struggle of my instinct of survival when facing death and consequent extinction. After all, isn't that tremendous fear something real that we carry with us always deep under our skin?

Such a part of my experience made me understand for the first time in my life and in a striking way the significance and the enormous importance of religion in bringing faith to our lives so much that I hung to it at the final moment of truth when I was in the process of my departure from this world. This has been one of the many important lessons that my experience through the process of my death produced in me.

But before this event, and in spite of all the efforts of my mother who tried hard to bring me to the formal teachings of the church in which I was baptized in Mexico, honestly, I had not paid her much attention. Not even when she took me to the Villa of Guadalupe.

I had another interesting experience with the image of the Cross. However this time it did not involve another near-death situation. Actually it took place after my experience with death when I was nineteen.

It was midnight and I was sleeping in the lower part of a bunk bed with my brother Guillermo sleeping in the upper bed. I was leaning my body to the left in the direction of the side of the wall and became awakened when I felt someone coming into the bedroom. I tried to turn my head to see who he was but I couldn't move a bit, I was frozen. All I could see was the blue wall in front of my eyes. Then I really got scared with the strong sensation that whoever he was, he was a malignant being and very powerful, almost touching me. His power had me completely immobilized and I was sweating profusely. But despite being very scared I tried with great force to turn my head to see who he was, to face that creature. However I remained frozen, feeling his presence very close to my head just watching me.

I remember that I had my right hand in the usual position as I always do, almost closed with the tip of my thumb touching my index finger so with extreme force I was able to advance my thumb just enough to make the shape of the Cross. I needed to do something to protect me! I was released right away and was able to turn my head as fast as I could, but whoever that being was he had already left the room in a hurry. I felt that he left scared in a hurry when I made the Cross with my fingers. After a few moments I recovered my calm and went to continue sleeping again with no explanation of what had happened. I was perplexed but I did not tell anyone because I knew people could have thought that I had only a bad dream or making up a story.

But the story did not end there. We visited Zacatecas to spend Christmas with all my family a few years ago and we were in my sister Susana's home in the kitchen talking with my brothers and sisters about memories of past times. My brother Guillermo was with us and he started telling to everybody a story about something frightful that happened to him when he was seventeen (he is two years younger than me). To my surprise, and I had chills when listening to this, he mentioned that he was sleeping in the upper part of the bunk bed that I described above, exactly on the same date and time I had had my bad experience, however I did not interrupt as he told us the rest of his story. He continued with the description of the situation exactly as it had happened to me, saying that he was awakened when he felt someone entering the bedroom, but that he was frozen and could not see who he was. He also described his sensation of the unknown being as dreadful and very powerful. Guillermo said he could not do anything but he felt the creature leaving the room all of a sudden. He also said that he did not mention this frightening occurrence at that time for fear of been ridiculed. When he finished I told him my story. All we did, completely astonished, was to look at each other with our eyes wide open!

I don't have an explanation about what really happened to Guillermo and me that night and I don't even want to try to explain it because this is the kind of thing in life that really scares me but the incredible coincidence should speak for itself. I tell this story just to point out how the Cross, which to me is the representation of my faith, came to my assistance in two different moments of my life.

When I speak of religion I am not referring specifically to a particular system of faith or worship because I believe that all faiths are to be respected for expressing the element of religiosity consubstantial to our human dimension. When we talk of the moment when the human being arrived on this earth. To me there is no doubt that took place when the Homo Sapiens became the receptor of its spiritual essence, the Soul. From here it was natural to develop our awareness of God translated in the element of faith and religiosity in humankind.

I would not judge which faith is better. That is not my purpose in writing this story. I simply want to refer to the anthropologic and historical findings in the long way of humankind on this earth that objectively point to the element of spirituality in our human nature to reinforce the point expressed above.

In the many artistic and architectural works all around the globe that have survived the eroding effects of time through the millenniums, God is represented in several forms as treasures of ancient knowledge about humanity in its origins. The most usual is the form of a sun, or in the times of the classical Greece and early Roman Empire as multifaceted gods, each one representing a particular quality or virtue they conceived of the essence of the Supreme.

Eventually, and reaching to our modern era, the most important monotheistic religions recurred to depict God in a more advanced form, adjusting our minds to the anthropomorphic conception of God with a human face in a human body. This way God conveyed His messages in different critical times for humankind through expected messiahs who represented Him and spread His word to the world. Our minds, as an expression of our human nature made of matter and souls, have been able to identify better with God when represented by a human God, the son of God sent to earth who looks like us.

Nevertheless, the constant common elements that prevail in the different authentic religions of the world are that death is not our end, and that the image of a supreme being as our Creator who is in Heaven is also our destiny. From their own particular angle they show God to humankind.

Several serious polls in recent years have established that more than eighty percent of the current population of the planet are individuals linked to one or another church of the world and believe in a Supreme Being. These are undeniable facts that speak for themselves of the important role of religion in bringing together under the same purpose the immense majority of the world population.

Based on such polls we could ask why religion is so essential to us. It is so important that without any doubt we could say that it is one of the quintessential elements that make us human beings, which is evidenced in the many testimonies and chapters of the history of civilization.

But of course this is not something accidental. We have been created from the beginning with the level of consciousness necessary to be aware of our Creator, and at the same time we can identify in ourselves that we share part of His essence. Obviously, we can do this with the understandable and evident limitations and imperfections determined by our material reality.

Religion is nothing else than our capacity to express our faith, how we interpret our human relationship and our purpose with God. This human need is achieved in spite of the fact that the different denominations of the world have been defined by their particular interpretations of God from their own temporal, cultural, linguistic and regional environments.

So we have many faiths in the world but all of them are valuable as long as they serve the high purpose of guiding humankind to its transcendental destiny. While we live in this world, they help us see and follow the image of our loving Father with all his superior virtues and absolute perfection.

A constant element that we can find in all of the authentic religions of the world is their common purpose of guiding humans on the road to God and happiness with the observance of codes of moral principles, and consequently the rejection of evil conduct. They identify the primordial elements of the essence of the Supreme, translating them as a model of virtuosity in their own religious codifications.

The framework of the moral life of humanity is contained in the different scriptures where they show their believers how to find the road to Heaven to fulfill their transcendental purpose. This is the way all the authentic faiths participate in the purpose of God for humankind.

Religion also fills the void that other disciplines of knowledge cannot or don' t want to respond to on the fundamental questions mankind has asked since the beginning of time about God. Even before I had my experience with death, I had asked myself

THE LIGHT AT THE END OF DARKNESS

these questions and had started looking for the answers. So can anyone imagine my tremendous joy and fulfillment when, in going through the process of my death, my eyes were finally opened to humbly find and confirm many of the same fundamental answers given by religion through the times!

However, I have to make the distinction that while my findings have an extraordinary parallelism with the conceptual truths taught by religion, these findings do not necessarily coincide in their description with those made through the lens of religion, especially with the particular details and rituals described by the different faiths.

Furthermore, the truths I found are of an empirical nature and extend beyond religion to the whole spectrum of our reality, including physical and metaphysical reality. This is why this book is not limited to religion.

But nevertheless, all the amazing and fortunate findings I made through the rich experience of my death have given me humbling reassurances of the importance of the teachings of religion in helping us to begin to see the Light of God while we are here on earth!

Regrettably, on the other hand, I could not close my eyes to the fact that some of the individuals who handle and interpret religion via their positions of authority in their own faiths have, on many occasions, been tempted and deviated from their main purpose due to some earthly interests. From here have arisen the many wars and conflicts throughout history because of the competition of some denominations to be the number one or to claim the rights of exclusivity in reaching the truth. This earthly mentality has driven these faiths on too many occasions to the contradictory ideas of the destruction of others who are seen as enemies for not sharing their particular views.

That mentality has caused much misery to the world in the past. But in our present days it is becoming potentially scarier because of the proliferation of extremist religious groups resorting to terrorism with the weapons of massive destruction so easy to get in the world market without ethical or legal restraints. The present threat to our fragile world peace is being caused not only by the very well known factors described in the letter of The United Nations, but also many are arising now by the corrosive, irreconcilable religious differences of some faiths.

Another dark moment for religion has been the appetite for power of some churches in the past which, in partnership with some unscrupulous monarchs, especially in the Middle Ages, supported them on their thrones to gain control and power above the good of their people. These kind of situations are to be blamed for producing the extreme reactions of the Enlightenment with repercussions to our days. This is giving ground to the growing numbers of agnostics and skeptics who, pointing to the attitudes of the chronic illnesses of some religions, make subtle fabrications to erase the idea of God from the minds of the people, substituting spirituality with materialism and cold reason.

Furthermore, history cannot hide the crude fact that on too many occasions religion has been used in a wicked way by some churches to support and justify mundane motives beyond its authentic purpose like political and economic competition, military superiority, racial prejudices, extreme nationalism, or simply to gain power. So it could be said that every time religion has been corrupted in its genuine and only purpose it has paid the high price of eroding its particular responsibilities and capacity to perform its most important role of guiding Man to its higher destiny. We should not let the jewel of mankind be corrupted by evil!

It is for this reason that religion has to maintain pure its high purpose in showing humanity the road to God, leaving behind in history the reproachable competition with each other on the grounds of religious rivalries and not falling in the traps of power struggles or corrupted interests that have nothing to do with its only one responsibility.

In the eyes of God no one is different or superior because of our particular religion, social and economic position, skin color, or culture. Religion covers one planet but with different denominations. However, its transcendental purpose is so important, especially in these threatening times to the fundamental nature of humanity and world peace, that the only way it will be able to help us today and in the future will be promoting a reconciliation and unified effort among all the authentic churches of the world.

Despite these historical burdens of religion, I have referred to them only as a background to give a realistic perspective of my own sense of religiosity. But again, I do not have any doubts of the fundamental support of religion for all those people who have not gone through an eye-opening experience like mine to define their own purpose in life to reach God with its instrumental help.

These are my sincere views about the role of religion that I wanted to include as a reference of my faith that surfaced at the critical moment of my death bringing to me the indispensable reassurances that I needed when I was embarked in the amazing journey to fulfill my ultimate destiny.

"It will never be possible by pure reason to arrive at some absolute truth."

> \- Werner Hiesenberger

"The intuitive mind is a sacred gift and the rational mind is a faithful servant. We have created a society that honor the servant and has forgotten the gift."

> \- Albert Einstein

CHAPTER 19

WHAT METAPHYSICS AND SCIENCE CAN TELL US ABOUT OUR REALITY

In view of the intrinsic limitations of science to help us understand our reality, I will try to add and combine with science the findings of metaphysics, a fundamental branch of philosophy. With this I hope to present a broader basis in describing what happened through the very interesting phenomena of the reality I experienced with my death.

Since the very early days when metaphysics was developed by Thelas as a fundamental tool of knowledge in ancient Greece and later consolidated with Aristotle, the role of this branch of philosophy has had several definitions. I will just refer basically to its modern conception, the study of reality transcending nature. With this conception in sight, it is perfectly clear that metaphysics is a superior tool of knowledge over pure science to explain the reality of our universe that cannot be separated from the notion of a Creator. The elements of our complex and sophisticated reality should not be limited only to measurements and quantifications with mathematics and objective experiments limited to nature from a materialistic approach.

Our universe is much larger than what we can see even with the most powerful telescopes. But most importantly, its underlying reality is integrated with qualitative elements that cannot be disregarded with self limiting approaches to study matter, energy, and space-time. Not taking into account the presence of a transcendental intelligence and harmony that shapes and govern our physical reality would deprive humanity of its most fundamental reference to make sense of our world and to be able to see beyond our noses.

Based on the approach of this more complete and integrated tool of knowledge with metaphysics, I have been able to reach a better understanding of several things that surfaced throughout the process of my death. This way, I can harmonize now to a greater extent the two different dimensions I was able to experience, my temporary material reality in this world and the reality I had the amazing opportunity to visit in my incredible journey where at the end my Creator was waiting for me.

Let's begin with matter. The first basic question to be able to comprehend our true immediate reality, the reality of Man in the universe, is to ask ourselves if what we see in this world as matter which makes the solid objects like our own biological bodies, the planets, the stars, etc., is the ultimate substance that makes up our universe. We have to determine if our reality is only material, if only what we can see and touch with our senses is real.

We can start examining our own hands with our eyes to see how far we can go with this approach. What we evidently will see is an apparent solid shape made of what everybody undoubtedly defines as matter because that is the interpretation of our brain helped by our eyes. They even have color, we cannot see through them, they seem solid, and we even can feel if it is warm or cold. But using our imagination let's pretend we are using a regular microscope so we can go further. This way we can see its surface which before seemed to our plain sight as perfectly solid now shows cells separated by spaces between them.

Incidentally, according to reliable calculations our bodies, the human body, contain approximately one hundred billion cells. Galaxies like ours contain an average of one hundred billion stars. And our known universe has one hundred billion galaxies. I find this proportion fascinatingly interesting. What could be the meaning of all this? Isn't this the harmony and symmetry that relate to the different scales of the cosmos?

Going even deeper to find out what is the stuff of matter we use electron microscopes and we find that even the atoms are units divided in smaller elements, protons, neutrons, positrons that make up the nucleus, and the electrons that orbit around the nucleus. We go even further and find that these elements are made of even smaller particles that still have mass, the quarks. However, we should notice that if we continue slicing the different particles further, what we invariably will find is empty space between them, more empty space in proportion to the smaller size of the particles which in the last instance are pure energy.

Experiments are already taking place with the largest and most powerful proton smasher ever built. The Large Hadron Collider, LHC, the new eight billion dollar particle accelerator built on the Swiss-French border, will try to find the smallest particles of the atom, the Higgs particles, and to confirm what now is only a theory, "String Theory."

The goal is to confirm that at such small scale matter ceases to exist and is transformed into pure energy manifested in infinitesimal small particles, dense concentrations of pure energy acting like strings vibrating at extremely high frequencies. The theory assumes that the particular shape of those tiny strings and the different frequencies of their harmonic vibrations determine how mass is produced and organized in material objects, first at the scale of the microcosmos and subsequently in our human scale.

So we can ask then, where in our reality is the solid matter which we see with our eyes and touch with our senses? And where is the material world which in our human scale we conceive as such?

From here, if we wanted to describe in a simplistic approach our material reality in relation to the way the universe and nature takes shape, we would arrive at a paradox because that immaterial substance in the last instance is pure energy producing harmonic vibrations. Like musical instruments playing a symphony, it produces a kind of stuff that looks like matter in the way we see it. But in its ultimate reality doesn't exist as such! Here is where science will have no other choice but to partner with metaphysics if it wants to reach the ultimate truth which explains the reality of the universe.

When we imagined that with the powerful electron microscopes we examined our hand which seems like solid matter to our eyes, we saw only empty space between the tiny particles of matter, that at the end are just expressions of pure energy. On the other hand, with the experiments mentioned using the Large Hadron Collider, it is highly probable that scientists will find the Higgs Particles, those infinitesimal small individual units of vibrating energy that become matter. The unambiguous conclusion should be that matter in its causation is closer to the conception of a substance that originates in another dimension, energy with the power to make the material reality of our universe.

Having had the opportunity of witnessing the amazing power of God face to face, I am fortunate to know now, without any trace of doubt, what is the source of all this energy that makes the building blocks of our material reality, of our universe, and us. Such is God, who, with his infinite energy provides the substance and forces which, directed by His intelligent design through what we define in this world as laws of nature, produced the stuff that our minds in connection with our brains and our sensory elements in our eyes, ears, noses, mouth, and skin, interprets as matter and space-time.

With some special exceptions, unfortunately this basic truth about the origin of the universe has not been grasped by many of the geniuses spread through the history of science, in spite of their grandiose discoveries and theories that have given them so much recognition for having impacted the way we live with the amazing technologies developed on the basis of their scientific achievements. Obviously the towering figures of science have not lacked enough brain power, and I say this with the greatest respect, however the whole problem is related mainly to attitude, their refusal to humbly accept at the core of physical reality the figure and role of the Creator.

Even now their followers continue to be lost in their own irony with the multiplicity of theories invented to explain the universe with the new exotic mathematical approach of opening the possibility of infinite universes, which would take us to nowhere in a never ending story of explaining nothing. If they had only listened to the champions in the field of metaphysics who opened the door of our intelligence in order to admit and consider from the beginning the possibility of a reality beyond our material reality. This amazing truth that stands the passing of time could have helped them take a shorter road to unleash the real potential of science to achieve more substantial advances and conclusive results in their search for a truthful understanding of our universe in its causality.

The same evident limitation of modern science in its self-imposed isolation from other sources of knowledge should make scientists open their eyes to work in union with metaphysics and philosophy with the purpose to humanize their own field. The value of this holistic approach is self-evident not only for allowing that rich pool of brilliant minds in science to reach more truthful conclusions with no waste of their privileged resources and efforts, but at the same time in directing scientific progress for the true good of humankind!

In my case, and I say this very humbly, I am convinced of the urgent need of this unification. The amazing journey through my process of death that took me to a different dimension produced a clear and solid awareness of the nature of such amazing reality. And it simultaneously related me with the true source that conform the material dimension where I came from. In such empirical experience when I became disconnected from my biological body, my mind reached an expanded level of consciousness allowing me to identify my Creator. Since I returned temporarily to this physical world, I cannot close my eyes to the intimate connection of both realities based in the same factor, God.

The other essential aspect of our reality, the laws of nature, which in their shortcomings scientists only touch on the surface as a given fact with their traditional refuge in their mathematical realm when explaining many physical phenomena, relates to their own intrinsic nature related to the Creator. Science does not dare to explain what they are, where they originate and how energy is directed by these laws in making the other basic building blocks of the universe. This includes matter and space-time, and the tools which the laws of nature use with the absolute precision in shaping our specific material reality: gravity, temperature, the electromagnetic forces, and the strong and weak nuclear forces.

Incidentally, this attitude of denial has one remarkable exception with Einstein who once said, "In learning the laws of nature, man is reading the mind of God." No wonder Einstein had such special inspiration in reaching his scientific achievements with his theories of Relativity. Besides the high intelligence he needed to formulate his elevated ideas about the laws of the universe, the other essential ingredient had to be the kind of special intuition which no one can develop without the necessary humility and sensibility to become aware of the role of the Creator. In unveiling for us such important aspects of the workings of nature, the mind of the tower of science reveals the connection he made with God!

But continuing with the line of thought expressed above, here again comes to play the immense power of God with his evident role in the creation, shaping and functioning of our material world. But in the laws of nature this power through the forces mentioned above is translated in an Intelligence that directs His energy with laser beam accuracy to achieve a desired purpose, the creation of a particular universe designed to host humankind.

Such Intelligence is reflected everywhere around us but only if we want to see it. This Intelligence becomes more evident in the higher manifestation of nature with the generation of the biological life on earth. First it is manifested in primitive forms, and later with the emergence of the Homo Sapiens through its

designed evolution in the bits of specific quantums of information stored and organized with the purpose of shaping our
bodies through our genes. These genetic systems stored in the
chromosomes evidently are intelligent arrangements designed to
process and transmit intelligent commands to our molecules to
conform the organs and functioning of our biological structures.
But amazingly, they give place to the creation of the highest form
of intelligence known in the universe, the human brain!

With this model of the transmission of intelligent instructions
performed by our genes in our bodies in the making and functioning of our organs we could try to identify at the level of the
microcosm a similar pattern to help us understand how the laws
of nature shape the universe.

But where can we find the equivalent of our genes in the universe? If we translate the concept of the relationship of genes-
cells and we use it with the most basic representation of mass in
the universe, the quarks-gluons-electrons-hadrons, and their
relationship with the atom then we can see how this group of initial particles, this first manifestation of mass not only represent
and transmit energy. They are also the conducts of energy that
channel to the subsequent scale the electromagnetic and the
strong and weak nuclear forces, which carry the intelligent
instructions, the information, to specifically shape first the protons and neutrons, and next, the different atoms, the building
blocks of matter and biological life.

On the other hand, the quark and its associated particles
have a complementary way to transmit the instructions they

carry. For being the first manifestation of mass they communicate to the macro scale the tool that will shape matter, gravity. The force of gravity is produced at the same time when mass becomes a reality. The evident result of such transformation of energy in mass through the quarks is the manifestation of that higher Intelligence in producing gravity, one of the fundamental forces that shape our universe, the macrocosmos which in our human scale we can see. It is the force which not only brings together portions of mass that condense and aggregate in stars and galaxies, and even in black holes, but also shapes space-time, the physical reality of us and the universe.

So one thing is clear when energy is transformed into mass. The same process produces the laws of nature through two different but complementary ways interacting in harmony in two different scales. With the subatomic forces that operate and regulate the microcosmos of the quantum world which shape the atoms, and with the force of gravity which is also associated with the expression of mass, but this one comes to shape matter and space-time.

What is also clear is the linking of both dimensions of forces unified by a common factor. The same forward movement in space-time that brings more and more complex aggregates deriving in whole systems, implying advance, transformation, evolution, with its parameters in the framework of the image of God towards complexity, intelligence and harmony, movement towards perfection!

The harmonic forward movement produced by these forces is

imprinted in the laws of nature. But such intelligent expression of energy that we call laws of nature, as we can see, with the arrow of time point to the same direction towards evolution in its highest form evidenced in the purpose of the universe, humankind!

If there is any doubt of the above then lets ask the men of science to give us a rational explanation of how it is that the same scientific facts observed in a myriad of aspects of nature converge into only one indisputable conclusion, the anthropic structure of our universe! This fact that is supported by unintended scientific data shows that our universe and earth are precisely tuned to have life and consequently, human life.

There are several fundamental physical phenomena occurring in a broad stretch of time and places of the universe. If just one of them would be out of the exact value and configuration our presence in the cosmos would be impossible. Just one of these factors out of its particular size, force or position and we would not be here at all!

As an example, we begin with the force of gravity described above which makes possible for mass to condense and form aggregates like the galaxies, stars, planets, etc. If gravity had been just a tiny fraction different all the stars would have burned at a faster rate not giving time for many basic elements to form. Additionally there are other complementary forces like the nuclear strong force that sets the basis for the formation of protons. If this force had been just a tiny fraction stronger it would have made impossible the formation of atoms--no atoms, no universe. If the weak atomic force had been slightly weaker, the oxygen would have been only helium--no oxygen, no water, no biology. If the difference in mass between a neutron and a proton was not exactly as it is, then all neutrons would have become protons--no chemistry. The molecules of water condensate differently depending on their temperatures--water, ice, vapor; and this is the miraculous foundation of life on earth because of their different properties--no liquid water, no chemistry, no biology. Our bodies are made up of eighty five percent water.

Even to a macro level the particular position of planet earth in our galaxy is crucial. If it were closer to its center the tremendous radiation produced by the dense concentration of stars would fry us and all the biological life on earth. The same would happen if our earth were located in the periphery of the galaxy (but ironically also for an excess of cosmic radiation which inundates the empty space between the galaxies where the protective band of magnetism that surrounds a galaxy is weaker to protect any planet in the periphery). A similar situation would occur with respect to the earth's position in relation to our sun, too near, too hot; too far, too cold. By the way, as an extra factor, if there were no moon, no tilting of the earth would be possible so we would not have an evenly distribution of temperatures on the surface of our planet with the four seasons of the year. It would be extremely hot in the equator and too cold in the poles which additionally would generate monstrous hurricanes making life on earth impossible.

And we could go on and on with more of these amazing

"coincidences." But the irrefutable fact is that the Homo Sapiens can be present on earth because of the precise tuning of these factors. Shouldn't this by itself constitute the most important scientific argument if we wanted to use only pure logic to prove it, to be convinced that our universe has been designed in its particular configuration to allow biological life and us to live in the cosmos?

Then the next question should necessarily follow, Who designed it?

What is really unacceptable is the simplistic position of a small hard core group of the atheistic scientific community who no matter what, despite the facts in front of their eyes gathered by means of the same science and their irrefutable significance, still deny that our universe was designed by an Intelligence for the specific purpose of humankind. Instead they argue that there are multiverse universes with their own different laws, and that ours is just one of many which by "chance" produced our life as it is.

The mathematical probability of that happening by pure chance is represented by the number ten elevated to a power of five hundred. The monster number that such a figure represents in reality is the equivalent of an infinite number, so it does not make any sense. The age of the universe of thirteen point seven billion years would not be enough to count such a number. The irony is that this kind of grotesque argument, which breaks the principles of the most basic logic and the same principles of science serves to confirm what it tries to deny!

However, we still can be open to the possibility that there

could be other universes. The dimension where God is waiting for us with all His power and majesty could be considered from our human perspective as another universe, a reality of a different kind than ours. And who knows how many other universes are there but this possibility would not follow the absurd reasoning mentioned above based in simple mathematics.

Actually, in our universe we could find one day in the future, what now seems to me a possibility, that the black holes detected in the center of the galaxies could be giving birth to new universes, baby universes. With their characteristic monstrous gravitational attraction they possess, everything in their periphery is pulled and engulfed by these incredible celestial objects including stars and planets. So what is brewing inside those closed doors?

But even if this more plausible theory can somehow be proven in the future it still should not be used as an argument against the idea of our Creator. Those new universes would come out as the result of ours so they should also have the same elements, the same laws and conditions in the creation of ours. Those baby universes with the possibility of breeding their own living creatures like us would also make them children of God.

THE LIGHT AT THE END OF DARKNESS

PART FOUR

OUR FUTURE, OUR CHOICE

"The highest knowledge is to know that we are surrounded by mystery. Neither knowledge nor hope for the future can be the pivot of our life or determine its direction. It is intended to be solely determined by our allowing ourselves to be gripped by the ethical God, who reveals Himself in us, and by our yielding our will to His."

- Albert Schweitzer

"Nor shall derision prove powerful against those who listen to humanity or those who follow the footsteps of divinity, for they shall live forever. Forever."

- Kahlil Gibran

CHAPTER 20

A CROSSROADS FOR HUMANKIND

We live in a universe 13.7 billion years old but humankind has been on this earth only two hundred thousand years from the moment we jumped in a gigantic leap into the category of Homo Sapiens. Another important fact to define us in the scale of time is that now the average life expectancy of an individual is only approximately eighty years. Taking into account these comparisons, we can ask what would be the proportion of the existence of humankind or the life span of an individual compared with the age of the universe?

On the scale of our material reality we can see that our planet earth is located in a galaxy with one hundred billion stars, the Milky Way, which is just one galaxy among the one hundred billion galaxies that our known universe contains. Some visionaries are already speculating that in the distant future humankind, with its infinite sense of adventure and counting on the appropriate space technology, will want to travel through our galaxy from one end to the other. However the time it would take to accomplish this wish considering that the spacecraft will have to travel to a speed close to the speed of light would be one hundred thousand years. And to think that this is only one galaxy!

With all this in mind we can try to compare the dimension of a human being with the magnitude of the universe. And don't forget that the universe is expanding with acceleration! With these comparisons then, what could be the relevant proportion of an individual? It is evident that we are insignificant entities compared with the tremendously enormous scales of our material reality. It would be like comparing an atom with the Milky Way!

But all this is for us to see what it represents in terms of our human reality in the fabulous enormity of the cosmos and try to grasp the idea of the size and complexity of the place where we live.With this reference in mind we could comprehend our condition as human beings in relation to the magnitude of the universe.

If we were to see ourselves only as material entities compared with those tremendous scales we would not represent anything of real significance. But if we were to accept God as our Creator then the equation should change completely because in this case the magnitude and the beauty of the universe where we live should tell us something very important and extremely significant.

The value of these comparisons is the amazing lesson we can

learn from them. With the enormity and beauty of the universe God is telling us something wonderful and sublime, the scale of the universe with all its energy, beauty and complexity created by Him for breeding us, so we can be born and live and eventually transcend to Him, is nothing else than the measure of His love to us!

But the big question that should be raised here in view of this amazing truth is, do we humans have the capacity to be aware of all this? But not only in terms of the intelligence necessary, the main question is, if we have developed sufficiently the moral ingredient of our human essence.

On the clear nights when I can watch the sky sprinkled with thousands and thousands of dots of light emanating from the stars and galaxies, I ask myself, an ordinary human being, as many others like me do, how is it possible that the hard core of the modern scientists and cosmologists, with some exceptions, who are supported with the fabulous instruments of high technology in their hands that allows them to peek much deeper into the profundities of the universe, don't react with the same humility and admiration produced in us when just using our eyes? I become dazzled by its beauty and immensity and the natural question that invariably pops in my mind is asking who created this wonder above our heads.

I honestly am puzzled when these privileged people in the depths of their minds seem not to ask themselves this fundamental questions and why it seems that they are not touched by these same subliminal feelings. Of course the simple justification is that because of the nature of the scientific method they shouldn't care about what defines the human factor and its deeper reality. This way they can separate nature from reality so they don't have to deal with the most essential element in defining it.

But at the same time that I ask myself the above, I also wonder if the feeling of power born in these people as a byproduct of the amounts of knowledge they acquire instead of opening their eyes and their hearts is what overwhelms and confuses them in facing the tremendous truths reflected in the wonders of the universe.We can get lost in the mountains of knowledge if we don't know where we are going!

Or, could it be that the high intelligence they are given as a gift by our Creator when used separated from our mind that connects the brain with our transcendental reality will never allow them to see what is in front of their eyes? Could it be we are beginning to diverge into different species?

It can be one or the other or a combination of both. But the fact that is becoming more evident these days is that the further the cosmologists can reach to the confines of the universe, the more questions they produce disguised as exotic hypothesis that don' t make sense and don't have a truthful answer.

I say this because it would seem that with the proliferation of new hypothesis about the universe the only result produced is a growing confusion that is taking humankind to the road of nowhere. This is the challenge because depending on whether we adopt or not the right approach towards our origins and purpose in life which are intrinsically linked to the cause and purpose of our universe, we are going to reach a crossroad in the future that either could take us to our true destiny or march us into the nothingness. At the end of the road, humanity will have to chose between a world of light or a world of darkness!

But of what future are we talking about? Is it going to be the next one hundred years or should we be contemplating the next thousand years? Given the accelerated advance of the technologies at our disposal like informatics, biotechnology, nanotechnology and communications, it would seem that we don't have to wait for the future.

It is evident that the mesmerizing advances in those areas, especially in communications and the internet, are already substantially impacting our modern society with the new reality of our times, globalization. Our kids now talk of visiting Australia or India as if these countries were around the corner, and have friends come to visit them from all over the world. Of course, we cannot picture young kids without their lap-tops and their i-Pods. When I was a kid my friends were my next door neighbors and my vehicle to explore the world was my bicycle. We can see how our world not only is becoming flat but at the same time is shrinking!

The fact is, our planet is shrinking because of the disappearance of mental barriers with the creation of the internet allowing us unlimited sharing of information and communications almost instantaneously to the most remote locations. Repercussions are felt all over the world with new approaches to commerce, the economy, migration, and health issues. Furthermore, a new global identity seems to be emerging from these advances in ethnicity, culture and regionalism, changing the ancestral worldly concepts in our human reference of who we are and where we belong. However the relevant question to be asked is if all this change is bringing us a better world, a happier world. That question is valid because it seems that the traditional idea of progress remains the same in our shrinking world with no clear direction and without producing a happier society.

It is a paradox that at the same time the world is expanding communications to every corner of the globe and producing more goods and services, poverty not only remains as a shameful problem, but it is worsening in many countries. Actually, there is a clear trend with the latest disruptions in the world financial system that the middle class is joining the ranks of the under-privileged. We have more poor people every day. Complementing the problems of the poor it is an increasing lack of accessibility to medical services despite the amazing advances in medicine. And as part of the paradox we have the coexistence of under-nutrition and obesity growing hand in hand rampantly all across the globe. Is this authentic progress?

Insecurity from terrorism is the emerging sign of our times, nourished by ideological and religious extremism, and as a conse-quence, regional military conflicts are erupting everywhere. At the same time the new world powers in Asia want their share in participating in the process of decisions for the world affecting the fragile balance of power reached momentarily after the cold war.

Making things worse, these new factors affecting the fragile stability of the world surge at a critical moment when the arsenal of nuclear and biological weapons grows without any effective control.

The accumulation of the explosive elements that define the current international scenario seem to be reaching a critical mass because more and more countries with irreconcilable ideologies and blinding interests are joining the club of nuclear powers with the potential to wipe out the human race from this planet. And if that weren't enough, all these problems are aggravated exponentially by the threat of international terrorism resorting to weapons of mass destruction.

Unfortunately, the main international mechanism the world could expect to intervene in maintaining the peace under this threatening scenario, The United Nations, at this moment seems impotent to face this vital responsibility due to its own chronic structural problems.

If all these were the only basis for the prediction of the future of humanity it would be irrelevant to talk of the next one hundred or one thousand years because the way it looks now based on how we are living would seem as though there is not a promising future for humans on earth. On these basis the only predictable future would be the apocalypse. Is this the grim world we want to pass on to the generations to come?

Moreover, if we were to leave the verdict in the hands of a dehumanized science such an apocalyptic view would not have another conclusion. With its methodology of cold objective reasoning it could take us to compare humanity to a system which according to the second law of thermodynamics (entropy) would establish that the order in such system necessarily should deteriorate. Of course if we were to leave our fate in the hands of the prevailing materialistic approach of measuring humankind the results would be not different.

But precisely for this reason the fundamental question for humankind has to be resolved for once and for all, do we accept the idea of God or not? From the honest response to this question that has been with us since we became Homo Sapiens, the foundations for the kind of future we want for our descendants will finally have to be determined. Do we want their future to reach real happiness based in the undeniable significance of our presence in the universe that points to a transcendental purpose with our Creator? Or on the contrary, do we want to deprive ourselves of direction and the capacity to build a predictable future in dismissing the fundamental element that gives its meaning to humankind?

Paradoxically, the ancestral debate in itself should be proof of the tremendous importance of the concept of God for Man regardless that some argue against. The pure fact that skeptical people dedicate all their intellectual efforts, and some their whole lives trying to demonstrate the non-existence of God, shows how important this concept is for them. I am an avid reader of science and I find it ironic how many references to God there are in the articles. Their authors tell us of new discoveries or new theories in science at the same time they pretend to have the authority to deny the Creator. It seems as if the ultimate goal of science is to be engaged all the time in dismissing what is in front of its eyes, the truth!

From this perspective no one could deny that the history of mankind has been made one way or the other around the concept of God. Beyond religion, philosophy, and science practically all the cultures of the world have an enormous portion of their particular history dedicated to the concept of God through their art as well as their music, literature and architecture. Even our own languages have been shaped by this debate with a baggage of terms like God, The Creator, The Father, The Son, The Trinity, The Light, The Holy Spirit; and in contrast, agnostic, skeptic, heretic, atheist, and all the accessory terminology like Heaven, Hell, redemption, sin, communion, saints, prophets, angels, etc. Just look at the proportion of this kind of terms in the dictionaries.

Can anyone imagine the size of the hole that it would make in the registers of the history of humankind if the concept of God would be eliminated? What would be left of our human dimension?

But it is time to finish that never ending and senseless debate and not prolong the discussion about what everybody should know by now deep down inside their minds and hearts based on the teachings of religion, honest reasoning, knowledge, deep meditation, and even our senses that make it evident through the simple observance of nature, the hand of the Creator.

We are reaching a crossroads not only because of the time wasted in the already too long debate about our fundamental question without having defined the road we want to take. But also there is a sense of urgency in reaching our decision for the accelerated advancement of science and technology which impacts every aspect our personal lives and world society in this era of globalization and instant communication. There is not a single day that we do not learn about some discovery or invention in the area of biotechnology and genetics with the potential of producing tremendous changes in the body or the brain of the individual. Besides what this means to science, there is the potential for creating real aberrations with unimaginable psychological and social repercussions if they are not applied under a strict moral and ethical framework of reference.

Because of the acceleration of events and the nature of the risks we could be reaching the critical point, an inflection point, of changing the conditions for our own existence as human beings. Leaving our future in the hands of immoral interests changing the laws of nature as designed for our integrated and harmonic evolution could be the equivalent to saying no to becoming part of the project of God materialized in our human nature.

The present danger of tinkering with the powers of nature without a moral purpose is that scientists could go beyond science fiction and create true Frankensteins. It looks as if science wanted to eliminate the concept of God but only to replace it with another God, dehumanized science. The problem then could result in the creation of real monstrosities that can contradict the elements of love and harmony imbedded in the creation of the universe and the human beings made by our real

God.

In our creation God made us with part of his own powers, among them the power of intelligence. In the whole universe the most complex organ developed with the laws of nature that respond to the infinite intelligence of God is the human brain. But this amazing organ that houses our intelligence cannot be used like a machine with intelligence per-se separated from the other essential elements of our moral nature. Can anyone imagine a super computer with the powers to control and direct the life of humankind? Another facet of the risk is the high possibility of interfacing computers in the brains of the products of biotechnology (bionic men) and genetics (clones). When these crazy projects are brought into completion in the future the few real humans left will want to get out of this planet!

However, what has been said before does not mean that everybody in the scientific community is following that road to Armageddon. There are many outstanding scientists who, not having lost their human essence and showing their integrity and a higher level of consciousness, are ready to admit that the latest discoveries and knowledge about the universe point to a transcendental truth behind them. Some others more willing to believe in the basic premise of the teachings of religion point to the hand of God in the creation of the universe. They are not afraid of plainly recognizing such truth and don't care about being criticized by the hard core of their skeptic colleagues. These are the progressive individuals who have the privilege of access to an integrated and deep understanding of scientific knowledge, and when the time comes for humankind to make its fundamental decision about what we want for our future, they will be in the forefront of the definition on the issue.

In this regard we should recognize one of the greatest scientists of all times, Albert Einstein. He achieved the most transcendental findings in modern science with the formulation of both theories, Special and General Relativity and opened the door for the development of Quantum Mechanics. Without apologies he made it known on many occasions during his productive life he had awe and admiration towards the Creator of the universe though he did not follow a particular religion. Having reached the pinnacle in the knowledge of the atom and the universe, Einstein did not have an ego reason to deny and denigrate the image of the Creator of the universe as many others of lesser stature do these days. With this humble attitude, Einstein opened the door to be followed by other progressive scientists in accepting the hand of God in the wonders of nature and the cosmos. To me, this defines the real value of his legacy for humanity.

There are also many ordinary individuals who, within their own particular beliefs and the nurturing of their consciousness, have already made their personal choices. The most obvious evidence is the happiness and internal peace reflected in their images and the quality of their lives. But above all, they direct their actions for the good of others, giving moral content to their lives. These people have direction and purpose! This should be the main goal for the rest of us in our actions no matter what it is we do on this earth to prioritize the good of humankind today and tomorrow.

But it is crucial to extend the need for this fundamental decision to all the fields of knowledge and human activity. What we are talking about here is humanity integrated as a whole, looking for the prevalence and permanence on the face of this earth and its basic essence related to God. This can be the start, but the whole consciousness of society will have to get involved in accepting this truth.

Of course this task sounds like an impossible dream if we consider how difficult it is to reach consensus in a world where debate and disagreements are part of our everyday lives. However it is imperative to leave behind short sighted interests and egotistical attitudes in view of the common needs and dangers humanity is facing these days as never before.

God created us because of His love to make us happy. Our destiny is to reach the state of absolute happiness, but such a destiny is at the end of a road we can take only if we want. It is not imposed on us. We were created with the freedom to decide where we want to go.

The freedom we are granted to make our own decisions is the fundamental piece in the capacity to express our will. Without that freedom and without our will we would be a finished product and our individuality and physical reality would not be necessary. God wants us to walk to Him!

In any case, the first step for humankind to be able to identify the road to its wonderful destiny is its willingness to accept that fundamental truth. Once this essential step has been taken, this road will be totally illuminated with the light from the image of God!

THE LIGHT AT THE END OF DARKNESS

Part Five

Conclusion

"God does not require us to succeed; He only requires us to try."

\- Mother Teresa

Conclusion

Life is a wonderful thing. It sounds close to the title of a very famous classical movie of the 1940's, "It's a wonderful life," with one of my favorite actors, James Stewart. It is about a young banker, who, having lost everything to the last penny and frustrated with his bad fortune, tries to kill himself by jumping from a bridge on a very cold winter night. He is saved by his guardian angel who brings him back to life to witness how life would had been without him, as if he had not been born, so he sees life from that angle and learns to appreciate how much he really had with his beautiful family and good friends. It has a happy ending and the man learns to appreciate the tremendous value and meaning of his life despite the circumstances of fortune.

Mine too has been a wonderful life and I value it greatly. I also learned about the tremendous value and meaning of my life when I lost it. But unlike the man in the movie, my death was caused by an event out of my hands and I was able to return because I expressed my wish to find a way in this world to show my immense gratitude for everything I am receiving from God.

However, looking in retrospect in the evening of my life I also ask myself if I had not met God at that fortunate moment with

181

death how different my life could have been. The most worrisome feeling is that I could have totally wasted my life by not having seen God with the clarity achieved.

I asked for only one minute and forty-eight years have passed so far.

But what have I done with my time back in this world to show my gratitude to our Creator? I have done what I figured was the best way to express my gratitude to God by trying to raise a beautiful family in the framework of His image. And in doing so, I certainly have lived a wonderful life!

But by no means am I implying that I see myself as a perfect person nor will I be as long as I remain in this world. I am certain that I should try very hard to be perfect on the image of our Father to honor Him, but I also am aware that what He wants for us first is to reach true happiness. Perfection will come after as a consequence of this. Having met our Father through the amazing journey in the process of my death convinced me that this is His desire in the way we have been created, that such is our destiny.

Yes we have a destiny but it is not an imposed destiny. God is granting us the capacity to participate with Him in completing our destiny together. God wanted to know if after being created entities of mixed substance of matter and soul we can develop our potential to transcend and love Him. Our love towards our Father is the substance that makes us of His own essence, that love can only be perfected with the last ingredient, when we express our desire to be one with Him and reach Him for eternity.

Otherwise He would not have bothered to create the universe

to make individual entities integrated with this mixture, humans, to evolve to a higher state of consciousness and have the capacity to be aware of ourselves and at the same time aware of who created us.

An important conclusion that emerges from various chapters of this book is that we have two elements of choice. One is our acceptance to be absorbed in God with all our dependence on Him. The other, the desire to maintain our individuality as self-centered and self-sufficient. For the same reason it is why in our final decision the impending outcome of the process of our deaths can have two different results, completing our journey with our acceptance of evolving into a new form of life in the realm of our Father forever, real life; or wishing to maintain our individuality as we are used to in this earthly life but ending in a different destination, the nothingness, real death!

In writing about my fabulous experience with death and the several aspects of life that relate to the frontiers of our reality, to the limits of my capacity and with all intellectual honesty I have tried to describe every detail of the various stages in the process I went through as vividly and clear as possible. My special attention has been with the description of the majestic entity encountered that I identify as my celestial Father.

Added to my emotion of the experience itself with my death and return which I revived and enjoyed to a great extent in writing this book, there is also a sense of humble accomplishment that makes me very happy for having encountered a total interconnectivity in the analysis of the many specific subjects around our human dimension. The ideas of power, gratitude, justice, death, happiness, effort, suffering, fear, and consciousness make perfect sense when treated from the perspective of such experience with God at the center of it all. My conclusion is that the transcendental and the empirical knowledge about who we are is supported by only one truth, God!

The same happened with several of the conceptual elements of philosophy, religion, and science which from their particular realms try to define our reality. In my own assessment I see with great emotion how these fundamental elements of knowledge interconnect among them as pieces of a gigantic puzzle when integrated with moral direction and relate to the empirical knowledge I gained on my amazing near-death experience. All coalesce in perfect harmony in giving us a holistic image of the face of God!

LaVergne, TN USA
28 October 2010
202632LV00001B/4/P